I0487804

The 12 Rules of
MILLENNIUM MARKETING

"Your Only Choice Is To Lead or Migrate"

Victoria L. Blanton

Writers Club Press
San Jose · New York · Lincoln · Shanghai

The 12 Rules of Millennium Marketing
Your Only Choice is to Lead or Migrate

Published by Writers Club Press
an imprint of iUniverse.com, Inc.

For information address:
iUniverse.com, Inc.
620 North 48th Street
Suite 201
Lincoln, NE 68504-3467
www.iuniverse.com

This publication is designed to provide accurate and authorative information
in regard to the subject matter covered. It is sold with the understanding that
the publisher and the author are not engaged in rendering legal, accounting,
or other related professional services. If legal advice or other expert
assistance is required, the services of a competetent professional person
should be sought.

ISBN: 0-595-09678-6

Printed in the United States of America

Contents

Chronology

In Chapter One we will Get a Plan with the new 7 P's strategy of marketing. Whether your company is in development, already on the market, and/or in need of recovery, an effective marketing plan will position you to achieve the results you desire. To survive in the new millennium, you must "Get a Plan" in order to get results.

In Chapter Two we will Make "e" Business "your" Business. Are you a migrator in terms of adaptation to change, particularly in Internet acknowledgement, e-commerce, and real time reporting? If you do not get connected, make electronic business your business, sell time, and set your clock to real time you may soon be "out of business."

In Chapter Three we will Design for the Mind. In the new millennium marketers must improve their knowledge of buying behaviors. In this chapter, mind positioning, mind stimulation, the power of words, and brain function concepts are introduced. In addition, we will define the 7 intelligences and determine marketing strategies for each, and introduce one of the new buzzwords, the "experience economy."

In Chapter Four we will Raise the Bar. As a marketer you should pay incredible attention to details. People typically will not challenge themselves or their marketing so you will have to. I share examples of companies that have raised their bar and will challenge you to do the same.

In Chapter Five, Marketing is an Investment; we will establish marketing as a sound business investment. In this chapter we will discuss the tactics that are being used for cutting costs but are ineffective and lacking in substance. In addition, we will introduce the 7 key ingredients and discuss the talent it takes to be a successful marketer.

In Chapter Six we will explore the disciplines of Measuring Performance to debrief success. This is implicit because if it can not be measured, it can not be improved. In this chapter we will discuss the measurement of marketing, discover the 5 T's of Tracking, identify two new disciplines that are paramount to the measurement of marketing; the Cost Per Result analysis and the Payback Axiom, and implement the discipline of measuring customers interests.

In Chapter Seven we will identify that Problems are Delayed Solutions. We will challenge problems and overcome them with the READY Discipline, and implement the Universal Formula. I have developed a 5-step process that can be used to implement the solution. The Universal Formula identifies and predicts the lease-up, stabilization, and/or recovery time of a real estate asset based on any available historical data on the community and/or market. Its application is truly universal and applicable to many other industries. In addition, since problems are not always the issue presented, I will briefly introduce a professional discipline of discovering the underlying problems and the skill of exposing them with tact.

In Chapter Eight, You Must be Willing to Sweat. Marketing is not an optional activity. Any company that wants to grow and produce profits must market. In this chapter I will reveal 8 underused and underestimated tactics that many marketers have disregarded because of the sweat factor.

In Chapter Nine we will discuss the Field of Dreams approach, If You Market, They Will Come. It is a fact you will improve the companies financial statement if you market. In this chapter we will expose the two most common excuses and challenge you to overcome them. We will also discuss competitive strategies and the importance of building marketing relationships by building a bi-lateral business referral network.

In Chapter Ten we will Train the Troops by getting a new TEAM. We must train the troops to become millennium marketers. In this chapter we will introduce the marketing strategy with a new TEAM training approach and ensure they understand the "why" of tracking customer data for the database.

In Chapter Eleven, Form Marketing Partnerships, we will discuss what it takes to develop a marketing partnership with the vendors that provide the marketing tools and services that fuel our success. In addition, I will define the vendors responsibility for you and list the items you should request in your MRFP (Marketing Request for Proposal) that will save you significant time.

In Chapter Twelve we will look at many examples of The Law of Unintended Consequences. As you begin to implement the 12 rules you will be designing slogans, campaigns, names, and concepts that will co-exist with your strategy. You can not completely predict how your idea will be received, but by performing pre-search you can reduce the chance of having a downside of unintended consequences.

Introduction

This book was written primarily for the marketing or business professional who is looking for fast and effective results from marketing. I have spent 15 years experiencing and researching the disciplines of marketing and I have found that what is usually called marketing is actually three separate disciplines. Those three disciplines are: Marketing, the discipline of soliciting new customers; Sales, the discipline of transforming those customers into buyers; and Customer Retention, the discipline of servicing and renewing those buyers.

The purpose of this book is to provide a solution to a major marketing problem. The problem is that when marketing professionals attend educational seminars, training sessions, or motivational meetings, they receive poorly defined planning on how to implement the information that they have received. The reason for the poor result is that three separate disciplines are combined as one activity, which by definition is too generalized, thus overwhelming the strategy to such a degree that implementation is nearly impossible.

The key to success for any marketing plan is implementation. I have perfected universal methods of implementation that are applicable to nearly all service industries. These proven methods of implementation are the 12 marketing rules contained in this book that when properly applied can deliver outstanding results. These 12 rules organize the marketing process into a playbook, which allows you to easily integrate new marketing ideas into your existing marketing program, thus readying those ideas for fast and effective implementation.

In addition to the marketing or business professional, this book will be beneficial to the many vendors who interface with real estate. It is an inside look for marketing, sales, and customer service professionals in all areas of business. Executives can use this book as a resource for participating more actively in the marketing function.

Marketing in the new millennium requires an understanding of the "New Economy" and its revolutionary impact on the marketing landscape. I have interfaced the "New Economy" topics such as e-commerce, the experience economy, and the time economy into The 12 Rules of Millennium Marketing. As we explore The 12 Rules of Millennium Marketing, you will be challenged to rethink the way you market. In the new millennium you will need to secure your marketing position. Your only choice is to lead or migrate.

Chapter 1
Rule #1—Get a Plan

"If I had seven days to chop down a tree,
I would spend six days planning it."
—Abraham Lincoln

In the new millennium we are faced with increased competition and the demand for results. Results are the measuring stick. Now it's time to beg the question. How do I get started? The basic consideration is the plan. Whether your company is in the early stages of development, already on the market, and/or in need of recovery, an effective marketing plan will position you to achieve the results you desire. You must "Get a Plan" in order to get results.

The 4 P's

First we must acknowledge how the marketing plan has developed in the past decade. It was borrowed from the marketing strategy of McCarthy; the four Ps are Product, Price, Place, and Promotion. McCarthy determines these four instruments as the controllable instruments of a marketing mix. Many industries including real estate, adopted this application but slightly modified it. In their simplest form they are:

1. People—The employees
2. Product—The real estate asset and its amenities
3. Price—The price of the units compared to the competition
4. Promotion—The marketing functions

The only modification from McCarthy's 4 P's strategy was the exchange of Place for People. Why did we add People to the mix and leave out Place? People was added because of the customer service; Total Quality Management (TQM) revolution. It was at its peak at the time and more focus was placed on company-employee relations. Companies knew it was crucial to their success to involve their People in every way possible. After all it is People who serve customers and customers who demand quality. We must have quality people to perform quality customer service. Since the pyramid of management decisions and control was also changing, it made sense to get on the People train. This paid off big for the pioneering companies. Soon it became popular to market your company with the key component; People. It was therefore a sensible and easy fit to complete the four P's marketing strategy.

The Field Dream is Results

Why did we rule out Place? In hindsight, because we had not yet discovered the trite rite: Location, Location, Location. In the new millennium Location, Location, Location is the trite rite that is no-longer brite. Before we explore what the new maxim of the new millennium is, how did Location, Location, Location, shape the marketing landscape and particularly the real estate industry?

First, the Field of Dreams strategy was reborn; "if you build it, they will come." In many real estate companies, Location, Location, Location, became further exemplified by the developers need to be first in the market. For the leaders this was a huge success. For the migrators it was less successful. Developers diligently explored markets that were either underdeveloped and/or had a promising future demand. As a result, many developers had hits. Big hits, the home run kind. And, many had misses, the strike out kind. The strikeouts are now sitting in overbuilt markets also known as soft markets.

Due to the explosion of the Location, Location, Location maxim, many marketing plans were unnecessarily revised, changed, downgraded, and in many cases abandoned. If a real estate asset or company was regarded as an undesirable location, budgets were cut and marketing was often the first item in the budget to be cut. Some owners sold their real estate at significant losses rather than explore or expand the effort to overcome this obstacle through Marketing. The upside to this is that many buyers of real estate with more marketing savvy were at the right place at the right time and made purchasing decisions based on other criteria. Location was not foremost in their minds. What to do with the location and how to market the location was.

The Location maxim is also referred to as "Location is rule number one and rule number two is see rule number one." It became an idea that everyone bought into. You seldom pick up an advertising piece, newspaper, or real estate publication today without seeing Location, Location, Location in the headline.

The location maxim drove and shaped the industry from early 1990's to date. But what is driving the new millennium? Results. "Results is rule number one and rule number two is see rule number one." Results, Results, Results is the new brite rite. Although it does not speak to the customer, it is the measuring stick for all of us in the new millennium.

Why Location, Location, Location,—the trite rite is no-longer brite? Because in many real estate development and/or company acquisition cases, the team members responsible for the implementation of the marketing plan had no control over the location decision yet are responsible for developing a marketing plan accordingly. By the time the marketing professional arrives at the scene the physical location has become the only unchangeable factor. If location is the total marketing strategy then how does the remaining (location poor) real estate in the world turn a profit?

Some real estate owners are scaling back the development and company acquisitions and are working on improving their current portfolio of assets. This fits with the Results, Results, Results maxim yet as always, the build and/or acquire strategy continues.

Those that continue with the Field of Dreams build or acquire strategy, will increasingly demand the more comprehensive dream, the dream of results. There are a few informed developers that have already begun to include the marketing professionals first in the location buying strategy and then designing a marketing strategy for the asset before they move the dirt or acquire the existing asset. This strategy is in reaction to failed or failing developments and/or acquisitions. Marketing is now being regarded as an implicit function of development and acquisition at its earliest stage. Many developers are not completely up to speed on what to expect from marketing because the marketing professionals are still producing plans from the past decade. According to C. Britt Beemer, author of Predatory Marketing, "a marketing strategy that was 100% effective in the 1980's will have lost 84-96% of its effectiveness today."[1] The marketing plan, sufficient to be included in a real estate and/or any company due diligence acquisition package should include the 12 rules outlined in this book.

Reduced to Sameness

Location will still receive attention in the minds of the customer so it should not become a write off. It is important to acknowledge that a customer may choose your particular area based on location but it is up to you to convince them to choose your location. Nearly every piece of real estate shares a location with others in a given market place. It is not uncommon to see fifteen out of twenty ads in a given market; sharing the same thoroughfare, resulting in a shared location, market themselves as the best location. When you market with this strategy, you have been reduced to sameness. There is no discernable difference for the customer to make a decision. The millennium marketer will find the differentiation and market it along with location.

In a sea of locations, where does the customer anchor? We should consider this important key motive but it is implicit to realize that most people already know what location they want. If Location, Location, Location is everything to the customer, then how does the customer decide on which location to choose when they have so many choices? The solution in this situation, as in all situations, is to differentiate. Say something to them that the rest of the market is not.

Be specific, such as in the case of real estate marketing: only five minutes from boating, fishing, bike trails, and water sports. Or 6.4 miles to the major highway and 2.5 miles from schools, shopping, banking, restaurants, entertainment and nightlife. Stating "close to" is not defined and not specific enough. Equally important is the fact that they choose to drive into the parking lot. Most likely it has excellent experience appeal (curb appeal is out and experience curb appeal is in) and/or exceptional marketing signage; all of which are components of Product. Location is still important for the customer who is moving into an unfamiliar city and is not exactly sure of where the best place to live, shop, eat, work, etc. That is why it is suggested that you not abandon the word location in your marketing. But using Location, Location, Location in the headline is out. Mentioning how the location benefits them is in. Leave the sameness up to your competition and take the differentiation route, which leads to results, results, results.

The New 7 P's

In addition to introducing the Results, Results, Results, maxim, I have added three new P's and Profits is the most important of them. In regards to Profit, Sergio Zyman says it best in his book The End of Marketing as We Know It; "debrief your success; equally important, and perhaps more valuable than analyzing and correcting things that turn out to be wrong is analyzing and building on the things that go right."[2] Often we take business success for granted. Rather than determining how the success was achieved, many justify that their assumptions were correct and do not make the effort to discover why it was on target. Thus, setting themselves up for failure at a later date.

Whether your measurement is the quarter to quarter treadmill of Wall Street or the measurement of an Owner's profit, the same principle should apply. We should increasingly pay attention to the successes. In a downsized economy it is the under performers that typically get all the attention. Challenge yourself and your company to get the under performers to perform by use of these 12 rules, and spend equal time, if not more time, with the successful ones to grow more profits. Many spend 80 percent of their time on the problems and only 20 percent on the successes.

Though the 4 P's traditional marketing mix is hardwired as our marketing Standard Operating Procedure (SOP), the adding of three more instruments will significantly improve your lead position. This leads to the development of a marketing plan with instruments that pertain more to the end game of results. The original four P's do not directly speak to or about results. They need to be expanded. This new rule partners with the rule of 7's. 7 instruments rather than four not only provide additional focus on areas that are closer to actual results, it also affords remembrance. By affording remembrance it is more likely to be implemented. Early studies by the telephone companies have established that the average person can comfortably recall up to seven digits. If you remember and market by the following components, you will get results.

1. People
2. Product
3. Price
4. Promotion
5. Physical
6. Progress
7. Profits

People is the first component of the plan. It is People that will assist in the development and implement the plan. You should train them to be marketers. From one employee to an army of employees, without training, a swarm of solicited customers will do no good if the team is not trained on the strategies that brought them there. In Chapter Ten, we discuss Train the Troops and how to implement the new TEAM training approach. You should keep track of which employees have had training, develop a tickler file of them. Also in the People section is where you include the information about any incentive program you plan to implement as a result of achieving the marketing goals.

Product is the second component of the plan. In addition to the importance of having a superior product and/or service through exemplary curb experience appeal, amenities, and ready product, it is equally important to have superior product and service representation in your promotional advertising. Attracting customers to visit your real estate and/or place of business is achieved by designing for the mind with memorable and thought provoking messages in your advertising. Including photos and descriptions of what the experience will be is paramount.

In this section of the plan you will maintain the product and service messages of your competition by including pictures of their product, copies of all their advertising and their collateral materials, such as brochures, newsletters, and Internet ads. If you are making product and service representation decisions without having viewed your competition's collateral product and service representation you can not ensure differentiation. This is why many businesses are marketed with sameness. No wonder customers are confused, everyone is doing and saying the same thing to get their attention.

If you believe the differentiation tactics of the past decade are still effective, for example: answering the phone by saying, "It's a great day at Happy Acres, this is Happy Acres Sales and Service Consultant, I can help you" will still get attention, just ask your techno-driven, impatient, highly informed customers to tell you why they do not view this as differentiation. That is if you do not get hung up on before you can ask. If you continue with the tactics of the past decades such as this you will lose market share because we have trained the customer to put up their "trickery shield" when they encounter these types of tactics.

Price is the third component of the plan and it also encompasses positioning. Whether you intend to compete on price or not you should complete an extensive, in-depth analysis by comparing your product and/or service to the competitions. This will include a comparison of all features and benefits. In real estate, we must compare amenities, floor plans, models, and all the administrative costs and rules associated with the application and the process, etc. We should also maintain copies of the competition's lease/sales agreement. Every company should have an extensive market survey and it should be placed in this section to support your pricing/positioning strategy.

Many marketers are unsure who the "real" competition are or decide for themselves based on the information gathered in the market survey research or they just go by the ones listed on the existing market survey. Challenge that information! Many market surveys are outdated and were determined by past staffs or marketers. It is not up to the staff or marketer to determine whom the competition is anyway, it is only up to the customers. If you want to establish who your "real" competition is spend at least thirty days asking every customer to name the competition they are interested in. It is that easy to find out and yet many marketers continue to decide who their competition is, in absence of asking the right people, the customers.

It is equally important to continually shop the competition. It is interesting what some employees may perceive as non-competition. When asked who their competition is, usually they answer with some degree of accuracy. But many times when asked if a certain competition is giving them competition and they are not one listed on the market survey they typically will respond by saying, "we never hear our customers mention that one so we do not consider them competition." The problem with that response is there is much research that reports that the reason they never hear the customer name that particular competitor is because they were sold on them and therefore never made it to your company. By getting out there and shopping the competition you will find out if such supposedly "non-competition" are actually competition.

Marketers are dedicated to profits and profits are derived from price. Price is an important element; however, it is not always foremost to the customer in making a decision. Although people are price conscious, Jay Conrad Levinson, author of Guerrilla Marketing Weapons states "in a research study designed to show prime influences, confidence came in first, quality came in second, service came in third, and selection came in fourth, price came in ninth."[3] The study also revealed 86 percent did not rank price as first. Using the data from this research study you would get 86 percent of the market share whereas a priced only positioning strategy would receive attention from only the remaining 14 percent. Be mindful of this fact when you are pricing your product and/or services and surrendering to the excuse that the customers will not buy because of your price.

Price, Sales, and Concessions—Evidence shows having a "sale" actually decreases a companies business. In the short term it would appear the opposite. As described in immutable law #11 of the book The 22 Immutable Laws of Marketing by Al Ries and Jack Trout, companies that offer sales are sending a message to the customer that their regular prices are too high. In the real estate and retail industry, sales and concessions have become commonplace. Those with more marketing talent have not surrendered to sales and concessions even when the competition has. The effects on the company are not only on the immediate financial statement but also reflect at customer retention time. You now have a reputation with that previously concessioned customer as a discount house. No matter how confident you are about your services and your renewal offer, if you are not armed with a discount or concession, the previously concessioned customer, is not likely to renew without one. This is because you have already set the standard at the beginning of the relationship by offering a concession, which translates to the customer, as they are "special." This is not just another term that the real estate industry uses for a concession, it describes how the customer perceives giving their business to you and will, in every case, demand that same "special" treatment at renewal time.

According to C. Britt Beemer, author of Predatory Marketing, a 1996 consumer research survey on consumer negotiation technique reveals that "the percentage of customers who try to get a lower price by mentioning other stores, whether or not they have actually shopped is 59%."[4] Keep this in mind when you are negotiating with your customer at renewal time. You should also be armed with a completely updated market survey and comparative analysis to better facilitate the negotiation process.

Promotion is the fourth component of the plan. This is the category where you list all your marketing solicitation items that bring in new customers. A good way to start is to identify all the marketing sources that currently bring in customers and do a brief narrative on each. You should also list any new advertising or marketing you would like to implement. List all the campaigns and programs that currently co-exist with your marketing effort. Their inclusion in this section should be reduced to a listing. Programs such as your customer retention program and other company programs should be listed but since their implementation is different than the Marketing discipline; the solicitation of new customers, it should not be described in full here.

Physical is the fifth component of the plan. It has been added because the number one reason why plans do not get implemented is because the plan does not include an action list. Since the new millennium is about results and it takes action to get results, you will need the new Physical discipline. Many times, the marketing items throughout the plan are simply documentation of marketing solicitations you already have in place, which are mixed in with your new planned additions. Therefore, it is difficult to distinguish the "to do's." The Physical part of the marketing plan is for the implementation team to have an action list of items that they or you are directly responsible for implementing. The Physical discipline is your "action" list.

Progress is the sixth component of the plan. The disciplines that will be introduced in this book that report your progress are the Cost Per Result Analysis (CPR) and the Payback Axiom (PA). Their application is more specific to the real estate industry but you can better extrapolate from this specific application than from a generalization, for your own use. One of the limitations with the original four P's was that many marketers did not implement the discipline of measuring performance against the marketing plan. Many measured its performance by measuring employee performance. Certainly, employee performance should be measured but not in lieu of measuring the actual marketing plan performance. The plans performance should be measured against the plan itself and in a controlled environment or the measurement is ineffective. Measurement disciplines should be performed consistently. Measuring at inconsistent times of an under performing business will only provide you with huge disparity in the data measured. If marketing is not consistently measured it can not be improved. By measuring, you know your marketing is making Progress. The instructions and illustrations on these two disciplines (CPR and PA) will be discussed in Chapter Six.

Profit is the seventh and final component of the plan. It was added to debrief success. Your financial reports with a narrative debriefing your success should be maintained in this section.

The Binder Set-up

The desired set up of the new 7 P's marketing plan, is in a binder format with 10 tabbed sections. The tabbed sections should be labeled as follows:

Title: The Marketing Plan for XYZ Company
  Section #1—Owner's Goals and Objective; and The Budget
  Section #2—The Universal Formula Worksheet
  Section #3—Regional Data, Area Demographics, Customer Profiles
  Section #4—People
  Section #5—Product
  Section #6—Price
  Section #7—Promotion
  Section #8—Physical
  Section #9—Progress
  Section #10—Profits

Section #1—Owner's Goals and Objective; and The Budget—Before implementing the plan, identify the Owner's goals and objectives. In this section of the binder you should include what the goals and objectives are or make recommendations in absence of them. It is not uncommon to have an Owner that has no specified expectation from the Marketing discipline. It is your responsibility to provide the Owner with the recommended expectation. Following the goals and objectives should be the marketing budget. It will serve as a reference.

Section #2—The Universal Formula Worksheet—Maintain the Universal Formula Worksheets in this section. It is likely that you will perform it more than once as time goes on. The Universal Formula will be introduced in Chapter Seven.

Section #3—Regional Data, Area Demographics, and Customer Profiles—In this section include and maintain regional data, area demographics, and customer profiles. The local Chamber of Commerce is a resource in obtaining information. Also your marketing and advertising vendors are likely to share whatever information they have. The customer profiles are your responsibility to gather and track. Usually this can be accomplished through software. In the case of real estate, the items to track are the business tenants and/or resident's place of employment, the city and state they moved from, the marketing source that generated them to you, why they chose you, and their preferred method of communication, i.e. e-mail, phone, cell phone, pager, voice mail, in person. This information is crucial in developing your solicitation strategies. You should train the team to input this data at the time of initial customer contact. If it has not been tracked in the computer you will need to review all current customer files to develop your own database.

Section #4—People—In this section maintain the People narrative part of your plan and each person's responsibility to the plan. A new TEAM training strategy is introduced in Chapter Ten; it will be useful in determining your people strategy. This is the section where you would also include any incentive plan information.

Section #5—Product—In this section include the Product and/or services narrative part of your plan. In addition, you will maintain the product messages of your competition by including pictures of their product, copies of all their advertising, and collateral materials such as brochures, newsletters, and Internet ads.

Section #6—Price—In this section include the Price narrative part of your plan. In addition, you will maintain an extensive, in-depth comparison analysis of the competition with a market survey. Maintain copies of 1.5 years worth of market surveys. Any less time and it will not be a proper evaluation of your price increases in comparison to the competition. Also by maintaining a copy of each of your competitor's lease/sales agreements, you can make a comparison and utilize it as a marketing tool.

Section #7—Promotion—In this section include the Promotion narrative part of your plan by listing all your advertising and solicitation items. In addition, you will maintain copies of all your promotional campaigns, copies of ads, flyers, etc. You should date each of them on the back and indicate the results for future reference.

Section #8—Physical—In this section include the Physical narrative part of your plan, which is your action items. Keep them updated as you accomplish your marketing tasks. In addition you should put your action items on a calendar to stay organized and up to date.

Section #9—Progress—In this section you will include the measurement reports. There are two new measurement disciplines introduced in this book. The Cost Per Result discipline and the Payback Axiom. You will maintain both reports in this section. The instructions and illustrations on these two disciplines (CPR and PA) are introduced in Chapter Six.

Section #10—Profits—In this section you will include the Profits narrative part of your plan identifying the profit goals. In addition, you will maintain your financial reports and a summary each month and/or quarter, debriefing your success.

Got a Plan
Now that you got a plan, you can continue to attend seminars, training sessions and motivational meetings to get the marketing flavors of the week, and still come away with an overwhelming amount of flavors. But now, you have a marketing plan format in which to implement them into. You'll need the rest of the Playbook too, so now it's time to get connected.

Chapter 2
Rule #2—Make "e" Business "your" Business

"He that will not apply new remedies must expect new evils; for time is the greatest innovator."

—*Francis Bacon*

My goal in this chapter is to familiarize you with the technology that is crucial to your success in the new millennium. Are you a migrator in terms of adaptation to changes, particularly in technology such as Internet acknowledgement, e-commerce, the time economy, and real time systems and management?

The Internet is the fastest growing media of all time and it is implicit to your success to get connected and leverage the World Wide Web for e-commerce and real time technology. If you do not get connected, make electronic business your business, sell time, and set your clock to real time, you may soon be "out of business."

Get a license to speed; 24/7

The Internet is another way to provide customer service but with the new paradigm shift to self-service. Just because it is not face to face service does not make it any less a service. Self-service once had a negative connotation but this is no longer the case. "Today's customers demand operations that are airborne, online, and in real time."[1] By being on the net we are available to our customers at their convenience not ours. Even today, amidst the Internet buzz many companies are not connected. In the new millennium it is crucial that you hardwire the Internet to your Marketing discipline.

Internet customers want premium service and they define premium service as self-service. You will be open 24 hours a day, 7 days a week; on the information superhighway. In the new millennium of marketing there is no such thing as "we're closed."

Advertising your company on the Internet adds to the quality of life for your customer. By being on the net your customer can do their shopping and research from the comfort of their home or office. The time they save adds to their quality of life.

Web sites should engage customers

Some of the most effective web sites include a virtual reality experience. You can implement this by giving a virtual reality tour of your product and/or services online. In real estate, you can accomplish this by including photos of the asset, amenities, interior pictures of offices and/or homes. Fully decorated models are preferred but in absence of such, a picture is acceptable with tasteful mini-model type decorations. This will provide the virtual reality seeker with a spacial perspective of size. Amenity and lifestyle are also key points of interests for the seeker. Download time is certainly a challenge but many end users have the advanced technology to expedite this process.

Virtual reality is not the same as being there. The missing elements of human interaction such as a smile, handshake, gestures, and body language, all issues of trust and confidence can not come across the virtual reality screen. Many customers prefer the human element as opposed to the virtual elements. Whatever the preference, it is your responsibility as a marketer to employ a diversity of Marketing disciplines.

E-commerce is the buzzword

E-commerce is not new but it is another buzzword for the new millennium. It provides the opportunity for companies to internally and externally exchange information. Such features for the real estate industry include electronic processing for rental receipts, processing of cash management, customized statements, and customized marketing, such as web leasing. You are a leader if you are implementing web based information exchange and commerce applications.

Features such as electronic processing of rental receipts not only is an added convenience to the customer, it affords consistent controls to improve efficiency and accuracy. Electronic processing as a banking function for cash management is not only an added convenience in terms of timeliness in processing the income receipts but it also affords customized statements and flexibility for the end client."[2] If you take steps towards utilizing e-commerce to increase communication, customize marketing to customers, customer rent/sales collection and banking, and an overall improvement of asset operations, increased profits will be the result.

E-commerce is particularly compelling for companies with online services. With high-speed access you can brand local content as another revenue stream. The customer will be able to buy directly from your home page. Such local content can include weather information, traffic, groceries, etc. and links to shopping malls online. This creates an infrastructure for people to buy from home.

Real estate assets will need to identify on-site storage space or build it as the mass movement to online shopping escalates. Communities with storage space will receive premiums from time-starved customers who work outside the home and/or their office and utilize online services for their shopping needs. These busy people are not available to receive their deliveries and the real estate "office" has much to gain by facilitating the delivery process in a service oriented manner by accepting the deliveries and storing them safely.

Real Time

The best definition of real time is articulated by Regis McKenna, author of Real Time; Preparing for the Age of the Never Satisfied Customer, "real time is characterized by the shortest possible lapse between idea and reaction between initiation and result."[3] It takes action and response to be in real time. We are already experiencing real time in our daily lives, for example using an ATM machine, a credit card, or by watching live television coverage. Because of technology we can compress the time it takes to disseminate information, make decisions, and take action in real time. Real time is not merely a system of doing things faster than before, since we experience real time in many ways other than technology. "Companies best equipped for the twenty-first century will consider investment in real time systems as essential to maintaining their competitive edge."[4] This can be accomplished in many ways, for one, by simply adding a toll-free number you are creating a real time system. The perception to the customer builds value but if your toll-free number is answered with a recording the value is near zero. Another form of a real time management system is to print your web address on your materials. This has a huge value run especially to the solicited customers whom elect to perform their own self-service research into your offering.

Real Time marketing reports are your silent marketing partner. A real time marketing system affords a marketer the opportunity to review reported marketing data that reflects the measured performance of the marketing strategy for any business. By having access to reported data in real time we can analyze the information, make decisions, and take action based on the information in real time.

Selling Time is Found Money

Selling time is found money in what I refer to as the "time economy." We are living in a world where time has become an economic offering. Marketers need to gain a better understanding of their customer's time-starved lives. In this supercharged market place, technology is so subtle and transparent that it is hardly recognizable. A virtual world has been created at our command. Time has transformed our daily lives and has become pervasive; marketers must concentrate on their customer's time in order to receive more high-profit potential. Customers "habits, attitudes, opinions, preferences, expectations, demands, perceptions, and needs all adept unwittingly to an environment in which immediacy rules."[5]

Your ability to provide immediacy to your customers by being a rapid marketer and selling time is your best competitive advantage in the new millennium. You must make it easy for customers to do business with you. Such efficiencies should include the following:

Online Electronic Payment—Offering a convenient method of transaction is not only a convenience to your customer, it provides you with a competitive strategy. This is especially helpful for real estate customers to use when reserving their home or office space. It is likely you will get more "sight unseen" business by providing this time saving service. The message you send to a customer by having a sophisticated and convenient method of transaction that is credible, often translates positively to how they deem the condition of the home, apartment, or the office space. The usage of online electronic payment is applicable to all areas of business.

Information Analysis—Time-starved customers want complete, sequential and concise information on your product and/or services. They are appreciative of your thoughtful preparation of all their anticipated needs. In the case of real estate, a brochure, floor plans, pricing schedules, deposit and lease/contract requirements, schools, government, and all information relating to the ease in a smooth transaction is paramount. It is not sufficient to just hand a time-starved customer a few miscellaneous pages of things to do. Respect their time and provide it in the format of a checklist and a "frequent questions and answers." This is a great time-starved tactic and yet hardly ever used.

Web Sites—You'll be selling time by having web site(s) and communicating your web addresses to your customers. Most company web sites are "brochureware" a first-generation web site with general information about the company, history, employment opportunities, etc. as described in the book Customers.COM by Patricia B. Seybold. After a brief visit to your "brochureware web site," your customers still have no idea how to do business with you. Your web site should be "transaction friendly." In addition, your web address should be on all collateral materials and part of your phone presentation. Also, it should be mentioned in the on hold message so impatient callers can go directly to your site.

Web Leasing/Sales—In a downsized employment force, companies should find new ways to communicate with customers without relying on face-to face service. It is possible to implement such an application and create a very close bond with customers without ever meeting them or in some cases talking to them. Many companies have successfully implemented such applications.

Web Leasing in real estate can provide an end to end solution for your customers. Customers will demand the ability to apply online, make payments online, choose their home, apartment or office space, sign all documents, click on links to assist in the moving process, which can result in revenue enhancement for the company. Customers want to have the ability to put in a service request for maintenance, check on the status, complete questionnaire/comment cards, and access "how to quick fix" items, thus not needing to "bother" the maintenance department. The possibilities for new revenue streams is endless. Once you make it easy for your customers to do business with you, it will secure them to a level of convenience and habits that the competition can not beat.

Establish Communication—You should ask your customer what is their preferred manner of communication; via e-mail, telephone, cell phone, voice mail, pager, in person, etc. By being sensitive to their time, they will likely buy the time you are selling.

Toll-free number—Having a toll-free number saves your customers time, money, and aggravation. It also implies a higher level of service. In real estate, on average, up to 50% of your customers are coming from more than 50 miles of your location. A toll-free phone number saves them long distance expense and affords you the image of a 24 hours a day, 7 days a week company. The benefit is better tracking of your calls (you can elect to hire a company to provide you with statistical tracking and analysis) resulting in better planning of employee time on schedules to accommodate customers efficiently and accuracy in returning calls, etc. Once you have added a toll-free number, as part of your time selling strategy, future customers will save their time by calling you first.

Geo Coding—This is the exact latitude and longitude of where you are on the web via a 6-digit navigational code which affords your customers ease in locating your business and to obtain mapping information on how to get there. Geo Coding is an effective timesaving tool that your time-starved customers will appreciate.

High-Speed Access—By offering high-speed access it affords your customers such things as the ability to efficiently manage their money online, operate a business, and communicate with family and friends. The demand for high-speed access (HSA) continues unabated. The demand is driven by constant improvements in computing power, digitization of voice and video applications such as web cams, and increasing mobility of users. Customers HSA needs are often full-filled at work and/or school, they have become to demand the same efficient and convenient delivery of high quality Internet services at home. HSA is a tremendous business opportunity offering a time selling competitive advantage and access to new revenue streams. If you win the race for the fastest connection you will win the race in revenue enhancement.

Immediate Credit Checks—In the new time-economy, you have much to gain by providing your customers with an immediate credit check. In this advanced technology, supercharged world, it is aggravating to a person with a good credit rating to have to wait even a day for your approval. Time-starved customers will flock to businesses that provide such time selling services.

Retail Commerce—This is an emerging trend. You can build out or utilize current space at your business to offer concierge services such as: event tickets, photo processing, lottery, specialty gifts, coffee, refreshments, dry cleaning, bill paying, money orders, stamps, faxing, deliveries, courier services, flowers, travel arrangements, etc. Delivering many of these services may be accomplished by utilizing third-party and e-commerce providers.

Value, Customer, Time

While average marketers continue to teach customers to salivate at the mention of a sale or concession, the best marketers develop marketing strategies that further exemplify the value of the customer's time. By doing so, time becomes the concession to the customer. They will reward you with their business if you sell them time.

How does selling customers more time translate to more profits for you? Using this basic calculation, you can determine that the average person works 8 hours per day, commutes for at least 1 hour to and from work, spends 3 hours a day eating 3 meals, and sleeps for 7 hours. This leaves only 4 hours of "discretionary time." For the calculation so far, we did not include any entertainment or recreation time with spouse, children, friends, or family. If we factor in at least 3 hours for this that leaves us with less than 1 hour of discretionary time in which to pay attention to your marketing offer. Marketers with the most "time selling" strategies to make the transaction fast and easy will carve themselves the most time-starved customer market share.

Convey your regard for the customer's time in all your marketing messages. Only when we recognize it is the marketer who really controls the customer's time and interfaces with it efficiently, will the customers begin to attach meaning to it. If you are already a time selling organization, you're millennium marketers. If not, spend the time to implement as many time saving tactics you can; selling time is found money in the new "time economy."

Internet Perception or Arrogance

A Field Experience…Internet perception or just plain arrogance? Recently, a friend was sharing with me their experience with leasing an apartment. Here is how the dialogue went. "Okay," I said, "tell me first how did you hear about the community?" He replied, "the Internet." I said, "Okay, which site?" He replied with the web address of the site. I said "Okay, you saw other sites too, right?" He replied, "yes of course, there were lots." I said "Okay, then what." He replied "I used a process of elimination based on what I wanted, the pictures provided, and the ones where I could see the community, models, and floor plans. " I said "Okay, then did you go visit any in person and if so how many?" He replied "yes, I visited six." Then he interjected and mentioned four were from the Internet search the other two were referrals from friends. He could not find the two referrals on the Internet so he had to visit those communities without qualifying his needs first. He actually liked one of the two that were not on the Internet but had enough doubt in his mind to rule both of them out because they were not on the net. He did not want to associate with a community that was not connected. He said "If they aren't with it in technology how do they operate and how will I get service?" This emerging perception comes from millennium customers who are questioning how your buildings can be up to code if you are not "with it" in technology.

I finally asked how he made his final decision and why. He said he picked the one with the best model in the floor plan he was most interested in. He liked the way it was decorated, identified with it, and was inspired to try to duplicate some of the look.

In this example there were six communities to choose from. Four advertised on the Internet and two did not. The two that did not advertise on the Internet were referrals from friends. He visited all six and first ruled out the two that were not on the Internet. He was left with four to choose from. After a process of elimination he chose the one with the best-decorated model of the floor plan that suited his needs. This is what is called ingredient marketing in action. It was not just the Internet ad that sold him. It was a combination of a self-service avenue to search (via the Internet) and the community with the best representation (freshly decorated model) of the floor plan that suited his needs. That is why you should not "a la carte" the marketing plan. All the ingredients work together towards achieving results. In the Playbook, we will explore all the ingredients.

Chapter 3
Rule #3—Design for the Mind

"Words are, of course, the most powerful drug used by Mankind."

—Rudyard Kipling

In the new millennium, marketers should improve their knowledge of buying behaviors. Basic trends in consumer buying patterns are not sufficient in determining the underlying reasons why people buy. Behavioral science can be helpful in determining customers thought processes. It can provide insight on positioning our products in the minds of the customer. In this chapter, mind positioning, mind stimulation, the power of words, and brain function concepts are introduced. In addition, we will define the 7 intelligences and determine marketing strategies for each. We will also explore the new "experience economy," articulated by B. Joseph Pine II and James H. Gilmore, authors of The Experience Economy.

Why People Buy

Positioning is what you do to the mind of the customer; meaning the position of the product/service. In this concept we are not just talking about positioning the product/service, we are positioning the customer's "mind" to respond to the product/service. "We must do this because today, customers are no longer responding to the positioning tactics of the past."[1] To get into the mind you have to present the information in a manner in which to trigger their selective perception.

The customers selective perception factor is when they notice something they are interested in. Selective perception is when you suddenly notice more of what you are currently thinking about and wondering why you had not noticed it so much before. For example, when you are interested in buying a new car and/or just purchased one, suddenly you notice all the exact models on the road. Selective perception works in everybody's mind.

If the customer's current selection state of mind does not include the need for your product and/or service, you will not reach that customer with your offer. For instance, in real estate, it is naïve to think that you will convince anyone who has no interest in changing their housing or office space situation, will be wowed by your irresistible offer and change their mind. By marketing a real estate asset you are not changing peoples minds as it relates to their needs but rather you are creating a medium with a trigger mechanism that reaches out to their selective perception. Producing marketing messages that directly speak to those that have their selective perception filter mechanism already open is key.

Another phenomenon is that some people believe in, "meant to be's." You can reach this audience without needing their selective perception open. People have often reported that the message arrived at the right place at the right time. It solidifies their decision and calls them to action because they believe it was some sort of a special message just for them.

The Marketing discipline is a numbers game. You have to put your message in front of a lot of people to hit the selective perceptioners.

Mind Stimuli

According to Paul Postma, author of The New Marketing Era, your marketing message can be increasingly successful if you use this scientific tactic: "There is a certain order, independent of our preferences, in the way we perceive various stimuli presented to us."[2] When using text and illustrations we are first drawn to the illustrations. This is why actual pictures and floor plans are so important in your advertising. If objects, people, or characters are shown, we are drawn to look at the eyes. Scientifically this is the second stimulus but for real estate (due to Fair Housing Practices) it is ill advised to use people in advertising housing. Next, we identify a signature and/or a postscript, who is it from and why did they choose me? In addition, the medium should include a tracking mechanism such as "ask for Sally" and include an invitation: "we at XYZ company are looking forward to seeing you by (a certain date)." These tactics serve a dual purpose of giving the customer a feeling of being wanted and it affords you a tracking mechanism. Then the mind recognizes the personalization. Using the recipient's name, addresses, and/or company name, or employer name gives people a sense of membership and belonging. Then the use of words plays a key role. The mind will give recognition to the use of positive words such as guarantee, proven, fast, save, time, money, breakthrough, and easy. Words such as no, none, contract, and decision, are negative and should be avoided.

The Power of Words

When certain words are used in advertising and marketing, they can be discriminatory, perceived as a promise or guarantee, misleading to a customer, and can have an unlawful impact when challenged under the right circumstances. In real estate, to avoid both civil and criminal liability, obvious words should be avoided that are connotative of any of the forbidden Fair Housing categories; Race, Color, Religion, Sex, National Origin, Handicap, and Familial Status. But the courts have ruled on other words that are not so obvious. Rather than take the risk, avoid the use of these words in your real estate marketing and advertising. The following are 20 words and phrase examples that I have recently seen. They are followed by a list of 16 more to be aware of to avoid potential "advertising" trouble.

Security—Using the word security can be construed as a promise and/or a guarantee of ones safety and therefore has been widely unaccepted. In the real estate industry it is also known as the "s" word due to everyone's fear of saying it.

Courtesy Patrol—This can be another form of promising security. It connotates "round the clock" patrol, which is "doubtfully" what you are actually performing. Avoid the use of courtesy patrol, and the word "patrol" in general or be prepared to explain to the attorney's what you meant by courtesy patrol if an incident were to happen.

Controlled Access—I see many real estate assets that are gated, advertise the community as "controlled access." How can you literally control "all" access? You can't. So it is wise not to promise that you can. Also, using "limited access" has been widely unaccepted. The advertising of a gate can be stated simply by "gated community." Also "gated entry," can be taken literally and therefore implies the exit is open and not gated.

Staffed Gated Community—As you can see this doesn't even make sense. Is the community advertising that the gate is staffed or the community is staffed? You should always make sure what you are advertising makes sense and does not confuse people, not to mention the security connotation this may be perceived as offering.

Restricted Access—This is another form of promising security and should be avoided.

Manned Guard House—This is another form of promising security and should be avoided. I have also seen it advertised as "Entry Guardhouse" and "Guard House at Entry." It is nearly impossible to insure the house is always, always, always, manned or guarded, not to mention the connotation that it is a "man" rather than a "woman" at the gate.

Intrusion Alarms—If you have alarm systems, they should be advertised as simply an "alarm system." You can explain the specific details and functionality of the system with the customer in person by use of the instruction manual on the system. By advertising such things as "intrusion," "panic button," etc. may get you into trouble if an incident occurs and the system fails to perform its advertised function.

Intercom for Safety—Mentioning you have an "Intercom" has been widely accepted but not with "for safety" behind it.

Well-lit Parking—This business may as well hold up a sign that says, "we want to be sued." You should never promise the functionality of your lighting. If it ever fails and/or you are not keeping it in repair, if an incident happens, you can be named in the lawsuit for failure to provide the "well lit" area. The Plaintiffs attorney will likely get a hold of your brochure and use it against you.

Quiet—You can't control how "quiet" things are so why promise it?

Private—Using the word private and/or privacy should be avoided. If you can not deliver complete privacy then you shouldn't use it.

Exclusive—A trade word used to describe a real estate community as upper scale, private, and for members only; all of which is not wise to promise.

Secluded—Similar to private and privacy, this word can also be taken out of context.

Children—Due to Fair Housing, the word Children should always be avoided. "Children's Playground" is a common manner in which to advertise a playground but it should be avoided. Tot Lot is not a proper term either. Using Play area and/or Playground has been widely accepted.

Walk-In Closet—This is very common in describing a closet that has enough space that it can be entered into. Customers who may not be able to "walk" into the closet may be turned off by this advertising statement. Rather it is wiser to just use "closet," and/or put an adjective in front of it such as spacious, large, generous, etc.

Jogging Trail—Again, not all users of the trail will necessarily be "jogging" on the trail. Be sensitive to this and call it an exercise trail, nature trail, and/or fitness trail. All of which are widely accepted. Let your customers decide what activity they will choose when taking the trail.

Small Pets Welcome including Animals Assisting the Handicapped—Service animals (which is the proper term) for the disabled are not "pets" and should not be mentioned along side another. This is another potential "Fair Housing" disaster.

Affordable—From an advertising and marketing standpoint, the word affordable belongs to the affordable real estate communities with specified programs for customers that qualify for them. It is not as widely accepted to use "affordable" unless you have that type of community. The real estate industry has spent much time and money to educate consumers about "affordable" communities. Using the word when you do not qualify is misleading to many informed customers.

Good Neighbors—Even the best applicant screening program can not guarantee "good neighbors" so why promise it?

Integrated Community or Diverse Community—Due to Fair Housing, either of these phrases or anything similar are widely unaccepted and can result in a lawsuit.

Additional words to avoid are: Adult, Religious, Sex, No Children, One Person, Single, Mature, Christian, Membership Approval, Race, Mentally Ill, Executive, Two People, Physically Fit Person, Family preferred, and Age. The source of these additional words is the Seattle Post-Intelligencer, in a "Publishers Notice," dated Feb. 6, 1999. This is not a complete list, which would be impossible to put to print, since new "words to avoid" are surfacing everyday. Whether or not your business is real estate, you should review your marketing materials to see if any potential discrimination or misleading representations appear.

It's a no-brainer

Jay Conrad Levinson introduced me to the right-brain-left-brain concept in his book, Guerrilla Marketing Attack. It is a no-brainer, and it is an effective approach in designing marketing for the mind. You will increase the effectiveness of your marketing if you direct it towards right-brained and left-brained people.

Right-brained people are interested in aesthetic appeal; emotional messages, dazzle, and "warm and fuzzy" advertising motivates them. For example you can achieve this with color, fun, lifestyle, sensory—the feel of the product in their hand, a promise, testimonials, and actual pictures. For real estate, in order of importance, right brain people prefer interior photos of models and then followed by exterior photos by way of exteriors of the buildings, then the amenities interiors and exteriors.

Logic and the sequential positioning of the message influence the left-brained people. They are attributed to being fact finders and problem solvers. You will blow it with a left-brained practitioner if you have errors in your message. Whether grammatical or just confusing in nature, these literal brained people will experience no emotional appeal to your offer if they have been tricked, confused, or led to correct your message. An example of real estate marketing designed for the left-brained is achieved by placing floor plans in ads, dimensions, facts, a clean ad, map, hours, and a powerful but logical argument.

Marketing that does not combine the right brain, left-brain concept is unproductive. To ensure you have your message covering both sides of the brain have someone of each brain type review the advertisement before it is launched.

Intelligent Marketing

Intelligence results in intelligent marketing, designed for the mind. Thomas Armstrong, author of 7 Kinds of Smart, Identifying Your Many Intelligence's teaches the reader about the revolutionary theory of multiple intelligences. They were developed by Howard Gardner. The 7 intelligences are Linguistic Intelligence, Logical-mathematical Intelligence, Spatial Intelligence, Musical Intelligence, Bodily-kinesthetic Intelligence, Interpersonal Intelligence, Intrapersonal Intelligence."[3]

In order to identify which of the 7 intelligence that you are most proficient in, you will need to take the self-tests in the book 7 Kinds of Smart, Identifying your Many Intelligence's by Thomas Armstrong.

For the purpose of comment and utilization of Howard Gardners theory, we will explore ideas and strategies to maximize your overall marketing effectiveness by catering to all 7 intelligence's in our marketing messages.

Linguistic Intelligence is the intelligence of words. People who are proficient in this area can be persuasive, entertaining, and instructional with the spoken word. The "gift of gab," memorized puns, jokes, and anecdotes are favored. They are usually drawn to trivia, history, and they retain facts.

Powerful use of words and their meaning and the use of puns will attract the attention of the linguistic intelligent. A campaign that requires them to participate in trivia, a treasure hunt, or a mystery to be solved will get their attention. Equally effective is an ad with as many facts and historical data as possible. The "did you know that" strategy is effective. For example a real estate asset that is over 30+ years old would benefit from a brochure including such things as "that was then and this is now," "did you know," and the historical background of the area, community, and how it evolved. Linguistically intelligent people will pay attention to this tactic and then pay you.

Logical-mathematical Intelligence is the intelligence of numbers and logic. People who are proficient in this area think in terms of reason, sequence, numbers, patterns, and they create hypothesis. They are drawn to solving problems, balancing checkbooks, and factual data with scientific proof.

Designing marketing for the Logical-mathematical intelligent can be accomplished by the use of factual data sequentially laid out and a powerful but logical argument. Maps, diagrams, floor plans with exact dimensions, and the practical usage of the product and/or service are favored. For example, real estate has much to gain by the use of a comparison analysis of the competition laid out in a factual manner. It must be easy to understand and sequential or it will be deemed irrelevant. They deem errors (simple typographical errors) in messages and content to be non-credible. In addition, such things as a checklist of "to do's" to lease and/or purchase a home, apartment, office space, or business; a move-in checklist sequentially demonstrating the cost categories and/organization associated with transaction will increase your effectiveness with this type of person. Also, having a complete package of collateral materials in a sequential and logical manner will score you points.

Spatial Intelligence is the intelligence of pictures and images. People who are proficient in this area have the ability to perceive and recreate the visual aspects of this world. They are usually architects, artists, pilots, photographers, and interior designers.

Designing marketing for the spacially intelligent can be accomplished by the effective use of space in an ad, pictures, and artistic delivery. Moreover, the effective use of a tasteful and current interior décor of your business. For real estate this would be the décor of your office and/or model and clubhouse that will attract their attention. For example, if your office, clubhouse, and/or model is uninviting or cumbersome, spacially intelligent people will be turned off. This is not to say that small offices, clubhouses, or models will not receive their attention but the smaller size space must be well thought out and planned to maximize its effectiveness. Floor plans that have furniture drawn on the diagram in the rooms gives spatial comparison and is effective with this person. But this tactic is not effective for all the intelligences so it is best to have 2 sets of floor plans. One set with the "sample" furniture drawn in on the floor plans and one set without.

Musical Intelligence is the intelligence of rhythm and melodies. People who are proficient in this are musicians of any sort. They have a good ear and can sing in tune.

Designing marketing for the musical intelligence can be accomplished by having music on at all times in your place of business. Real estate benefits from having music on in the office, clubhouse, amenities, and models. And if you can put a slogan or phrase to music it will attract their attention. You should always have music on, even in a vacant home, apartment, or office space. An inexpensive clock radio is sufficient. You should also consider designing a theme song for your business, market it to your customers "on hold," and it will be impossible to forget you.

Bodily-kinesthetic Intelligence is the intelligence of the physical being. People who are proficient in this area have talent in physical movements and handling objects. They are usually athletes, craftsman, mechanics, or surgeons. They enjoy physical activities such as biking, swimming, boating, and those with especially tactile sensitivity enjoy fabrics, designing with them, and sewing.

Designing marketing for the bodily-kinesthetic intelligent can be accomplished by communicating the physical aspects and activities offered as a result of doing business with you. For example, list all the amenities and programs at your place of business and their benefits. Offer classes and competitive events. They are always seeking to hone their skills. Keep them active and engaged and you will keep them as your customer.

Interpersonal Intelligence is the intelligence of people and responsiveness to the moods, intentions, and desires of others. People who are proficient in this area are event planners, negotiators, human resources, teachers, directors, and Doctors.

Designing marketing for the interpersonal intelligence is accomplished by a display of harmony and kinship in your messages. They will be impressed with community involvement; self help offerings, and charity events. For example, you can mention local community events, charitable contribution opportunities, and include improvement classes as part of your offer.

Intrapersonal Intelligence is the intelligence of the inner self. People who are proficient in this area have a strong sense of their being and emotions. They are usually counselors, theorists, and psychologists. They are independent and goal directed.

Designing marketing for the intrapersonal intelligence can be accomplished by catering to a sense of lifestyle with ease, comfort, convenience, and an escape from the norm. For example, you will capture the attention of the intrapersonal intelligence by offering a place of solitude, comfort, and a relaxing environment. Opportunities in real estate come from offering a comfortable patio or balcony, Jacuzzi, sauna, a serene nature trail, or a tranquil view, all of which will be of particular interest.

Now that we have explored the 7 kinds of intelligence, and translated them into design for the mind marketing ideas, you will be better prepared to design marketing for many minds. Since you will not get the opportunity to have your customers take the self-test to determine their intelligence, you can however reach all of them by designing marketing that incorporates the 7 intelligence's in a variety of your marketing.

I would be remiss if I did not encourage you to purchase Thomas Armstrong's masterpiece book for a complete look at this concept and to reveal your "intelligent" proficiencies.

The New Experience Economy

B. Joseph Pine II and James H. Gilmore, authors of The Experience Economy, articulate that "experiences" create economic value. I believe in creating "experiences" through marketing for the mind and it too can create economic value. Pine and Gilmore describe the experience economy as an offering to the customer that exceeds the standard expectations of customers and engages them with an experience that allows you to connect with them in a personal and memorable way. The experience economy is not just about goods and services but rather providing customers with an experience. "When a person buys a service, he purchases a set of intangible activities carried out on his behalf. But when he buys an experience, he pays to spend time enjoying a series of memorable events that a company stages."[4] Experiences do not have to only be entertaining in nature, although entertainment is one aspect of achieving an experience. Companies should stage memorable experiences and connect with their customers before the competition arrives with a competitive experience offering.

Service industries have much to gain by leading the new experience economy. Those that choose to lead rather than migrate will create the new rules for staging customer experiences since there is no hard-and-fast rules to follow yet because this economic offering is in its earliest stages. Nonetheless, those that do, stand a good chance of success by taking action now. Pine and Gilmore report that the "businesses that regulate themselves to the diminishing world of goods and services will be rendered irrelevant."[5]

According to Pine and Gilmore, you can accomplish rich, compelling, and engaging experiences with 4 aspects of an experience. For the purpose of comment, I included the 4 aspects of the experience economy into a "design for the mind" tool. The 4 aspects are: the esthetic aspect, the escapist aspect, the educational aspect, and the entertainment aspect.[6]

The esthetic aspect is accomplished by describing what type of environment they will experience when they visit, such as the architecture, i.e. Mediterranean, gothic, colonial, etc. Let them know how inviting and comfortable it will be by marketing to their hidden need to have a place to "relax." Discuss the exterior gathering spaces and interior areas. Tune them into what their "personal space" will be like. In esthetic experiences individuals will become immersed in the moment.

The escapist aspect is accomplished by engaging them into activities. Let the solicited customer know what the "thrill" will be in association with your product an/or services. Also you will need to satisfy their interest in knowing what to do if they participate. They will want to be prepared.

The educational aspect is accomplished by marketing with the active aspect. Tell them what type of events will unfold before them. Let the solicited customer know it requires their participation. Inform them of the potential for newly acquired activities, knowledge, and skills. This can be accomplished by offering events and classes in a variety of topics or informing them via recommendations.

The entertainment aspect is self-explanatory. Let the solicited customer know what you can do to provide them with entertainment and engage the customer by explaining how they can have more fun, and memorable times by associating themselves with your product and/or service offering.

Now that we have explored the 7 kinds of intelligent marketing and the 4 aspects of the new experience economy, you can develop your Marketing discipline with more effectiveness. The Experience Economy by B. Joseph Pine II and James H. Gilmore, and 7 Kinds of Smart: Identifying Your Many Intelligences by Thomas Armstrong, will serve as your desktop companion as you embark on this new revolutionary marketing landscape. I highly recommend you consider adding them to your marketing library.

When you are on a limited marketing budget, you may not have the luxury of doing very specific "target" audience marketing. For example, on a limited budget it is nearly impossible to design 10 different brochures, ads, direct mailers, postcards, etc. to specific targeted audiences to generate customers to your business. By designing marketing for the mind you will accomplish a new kind of target marketing thus reaching a more vast audience. And it is much more affordable. Also by designing for the mind, customers with their selective perception triggered will first receive and recognize your message and then identify with the content, which greatly increases its effectiveness. In addition, designing specific targeted marketing in real estate can get you into Fair Housing trouble if it is blatant and obvious that you are trying to attract a certain person and/or profile. Such tactics are also against the rules in many "affordable" real estate communities.

All marketing professionals have much to gain by designing marketing for the mind. It is a low cost, low risk, and effective manner in which to solicit new customers to your business for maximum results.

Chapter 4
Rule #4—Raise the Bar

"We aim above the mark to hit the mark."
—Ralph Waldo Emerson

One of the greatest challenges in today's competitive market place is to continue to raise the bar. As a millennium marketer you should pay incredible attention to detail. It is your responsibility to set the level of expectation in which everyone can aspire to meet and exceed. If you implement rule #4 successfully, you will be paid back with not just having expectations met but having expectations exceeded. You should challenge everything even the most insignificant of things. People typically will not challenge themselves or their marketing so you will have to. Many times they are working hard but it is up to you to make them work smart. Motivate them to raise their height of thinking. Motivate them to raise the bar.

How do you raise the bar in marketing? Simply, by setting the expectation level and leading by example. Pay incredible attention to detail and demand everyone around you does the same.

Dinosaurs with Cobwebs

A Field Experience...I was at a community to perform a marketing audit and train the new team. I had arrived late in the afternoon and went to the office to get prepared for the days ahead. I was making calls and had to fax something. I was shocked when I saw the condition of the fax. At first glance I thought it was a dinosaur with cobwebs. But it worked, sort of, so I used it and went about my business. Then I had the need to use the copier. At first glance I thought it was another dinosaur but with bigger cobwebs. But it worked, sort of, so I used it and went about my business. Soon, the staff left for the day but my work had just begun. I stayed late cleaning the fax and the copier and all the other office equipment. I found knobs that were labeled "broke." When I cleaned them they worked again and the equipment looked presentable.

The next day the staff came in and thought I went out and bought brand new office equipment for them. Nobody realized it was the same equipment until I told them. Even after that, they questioned it because they said, "it can't be, that knob was broken." Not only were they impressed by my attention detail, they were equally impressed that I stayed late to clean everything. Everyone was excited about their new toys. From that day forward I received nothing but the utmost quality and attention to detail from this team. This experience heightened their thinking. It made them all want to do better and be better. In the days to follow, I saw much more care and attention given to the office equipment and more importantly the customers.

At this particular community since many of the current customers enjoyed the convenience of utilizing the office equipment to fax documents, make copies, etc. we wanted to expand upon these services but in order to effectively market this service we had to bring it up to a new standard. The customers thought the equipment was new. I heard one say, "Wow, it's about time, thanks, my copies look better." As a result we effectively marketed the additional services.

Although it may be unnecessary to wipe off office equipment everyday, this team did. They did it because it was a symbol of pride. You can get heightened thinking and motivate people to raise the bar by being the leader and setting the example thus resulting in marketing opportunities.

If you are frustrated with why your level of expectation is not being met maybe it is because it has not been adequately set and communicated.

You can not assume people know what to do, how to do it, and to what level unless you show and tell them. It is much easier for them if they have the rules and guidelines and the level of expectation to aspire to.

Horse-head hitching posts

The next two examples in raising the bar come from Disney. Tom Connellan, the author of Inside the Magic Kingdom; Seven Key's to Disney's Success, writes about the horse-head hitching posts that line Main Street in Disney. There are high wear points on the horse-head hitching posts and they get stripped down and repainted each night. In order to be painted and completely dry by the time the park opens the next day, the actual starting time is determined by the temperature and humidity conditions.

23-karat gold leaf paint

The second example, also from Tom Connellan's book, is the importance of recognizing the unseen things. He writes about the paint on the carousel. "Each part that is supposed to be colored gold has been painted with 23-karat gold leaf paint. Not just gold colored paint, but 23-karat gold leaf paint."[1] The kids and parents certainly can not tell the difference and neither can most cast members. But the cast members know it is 23-karat gold leaf paint and it serves as an important symbol. The guest are the true gold and even though the cleaning of the carousel and the grounds is not a pleasant job, the cast members are reminded of the real gold, the guests, and clean up becomes more worthwhile.

A Virgin's Honor

This next example comes from Sam Hill and Glenn Rifkin, co-authors of Radical Marketing. Richard Branson the Owner and CEO of Virgin Atlantic Airlines raised the bar with his employees when a competitor tried to discredit the company. British Airways, a rival competitor of Virgin, initiated a mud throwing campaign. Branson found out and filed a lawsuit and it was later settled for more than $900,000. "Branson gave the money to his employees and sent out this note: Thank You all for your help in our defense. After all, a Virgin's honor is her most prized possession."[2]

We can learn a lot from the Grateful Dead

Another example from Sam Hill and Glenn Rifkins book Radical Marketing, involves the Grateful Dead who are champions at raising the bar with not just their fans but also their employees. Since its evolution in the Psychedelic 1960's this band had a thirty-year run as a rock icon without producing a number one hit or album. The death of Jerry Garcia in 1995, their music and spiritual leader, marked the end for the band but Grateful Dead Productions still thrives and the band lives on. In order to keep the value proposition, the band needed to reinvent themselves again. They started a combination fan magazine and catalog to choose among more than 500 Grateful Dead items. Merchandise sales reached more than 8 million dollars in 1998. A fraction of the 60 million dollars that all Grateful Dead items generate for the band each year.

The Dead were successful at hiring and retaining a talented road crew who played more than eighty concert dates a year for thirty years and as a result "the band developed unparalleled expertise in the marketing, promotion, and execution of musical events."[3] Even after the group disbanded the Dead retained their loyal employees and utilized their talent to develop new revenue streams.

The Grateful Deads ability to retain their loyal employees was mainly by communicating what its product would be, who its audience was, and setting the expectation level by raising the bar in the music industry. Their brand therefore became more than the product, it was a relationship with their customer and employees. The Grateful Dead are noted as the first rock band to offer profit sharing for their employees. They also offered children play areas backstage for employees and guests at events. "Like other great radical marketers, the Dead understood the value of employees who shared the enthusiasm for the product and would in effect represent the company to the customers."[4]

While other bands hired crews for the duration of a tour, the Dead simply could not leave the delivery of their product to amateurs.

The number one reason why employees leave companies is due to lack of training and communication. Setting the expectation level and raising the bar is a form of training and communication. Raise the bar by setting the expectation level and you will experience a decrease in employee turnover.

To succeed in the new millennium you should not only be on the customer's pulse but your competitions pulse too. It is likely that your competition will begin to react to your strategies. Some by counter-acting your effort by throwing mud such as in the Virgin Airlines and British Airways example. When the competition gets fierce, it is not wise to throw mud back. Raise the bar instead.

Chapter 5
Rule #5—Marketing is an Investment

"There are in fact two things, science and opinion;
the former begets knowledge, the latter ignorance."

—*Hippocrates*

If marketing continues to be viewed as a non-essential business discipline it will continue to be cut. By cutting or scaling back marketing, it drastically reduces its effectiveness and in many cases invites further costs. In this chapter we will discuss the tactics that are being used in real estate for cutting costs but are considered fluff puff, ineffective and lacking in substance. The common phrase "you have to spend money to make money" holds true in marketing any business if you plan to achieve results. In addition, we will introduce the 7 key ingredients and discuss the talent it takes to be a successful marketer. Professional marketers are part of the investment equation. "By establishing marketing as a sound business investment marketers can get the kind of resources they need to do their jobs more effectively."[1]

Marketing is about systematically coming up with a strategy, designing a plan, creating tools, and putting them into action, but with whose money? The investor's money. The investor in this case is the person with whom you need to get approval from to invest in your plan so you can implement it. It may be a budget supervisor, the Owner and/or investor of the asset or business. Regardless of who it is, if you regard marketing as an investment rather than an expense, it is likely you will get the investment funds you need to support your program.

The millennium marketer will be improving the business by, improving the marketing, by investing in marketing.

The FP Factor

Many real estate professionals have marketed with fluff puff stuff; I call the FP Factor. The fluff puff factor is defined as a marketing tactic that is a low cost investment, generates some excitement but lacks substance, which usually results in loss of credibility especially when used for the wrong target audience. An example of a real estate fluff puff tactic is the use of a blow up doll or balloons placed in the bathtub of vacant homes and/or apartments. Or excessive use of decorations such as party favors, balloons, notes in the cabinets and closets, and cutouts of feet taped to the floor. The millennium customer is not looking for a space to throw a party in and they do not need a tracking device to find their way from the kitchen to the bathroom or office to office. They are looking for a new home and/or office with substance. Feet taped to the floor and balloons in the tub are not substance. These types of FP tactics are thought to be a low cost alternative to the mini-model concept. Businesses with budgeting challenges utilize these FP tactics in argument that it is all they can afford. The price to put together a FP party favor theme in your place of business is low but the cost is high, meaning it costs you valuable business.

FP marketing tactics once thought of as a differentiation tactic or "remember us" tactic is wasted dollars no matter how inexpensive they are. Use your marketing dollars more wisely and set up a mini-model (no furniture) of tasteful kitchen and bath items for homes or office type decorations that a customer would identify with. Research studies indicate that distracting visual aids in a sales presentation actually cause the customer to show disinterest in a product by not identifying with the visual aid. They focus on the visual aid rather than the product or service and therefore have a hard time making the transformation back to "what does this have to do with me." Party favor decorations have also been known to impair the customer's ability to visually picture themselves living or working in that space. The key to an effective presentation with a customer is to get them to visualize living and/or working in that space. Party favors get in the way of that and many times, when over decorated, the space will appear to be smaller. It's a matter of providing more substance and substance brings more results.

In the retail industry, proper merchandising of products is essential. Use of holiday themes is common and often very successful. If your product and/or service have a seasonal advantage that allows for maximum marketing to new customers as a result of a holiday theme, then I recommend your making the investment in those type "decorations." However, keep in mind the time-table of how long you can use the decorations. In marketing, for most holidays, it is considered "tacky" to still have holiday decorations displayed as early as the first day after the holiday.

Millennium customers are informed and they want substance. Many will view your FP as "trickery" and resent it. As tempting as the FP may be, these tactics will not measure up in the new millennium of marketing. I align the FP Factor with the Law of Hype—"People and institutions whose surface value (hype) is less than their substance will be driven out by those of whom the reverse is true."[2]

While many others were caught up in the FP tactics, I was asking the customer at the point of purchase what really caused them to visit and then buy from me. It was not the FP tactics displayed by the competition. It was the substance we provided and the ability to identify with the targeted space by way of the model and vacant apartment home, then visualize living in it.

Another form of FP tactics is funny slogans and/or jokes in ads. Many times customers do not get the jokes because they do not know the "business" or they do not make the connection. According to Jay Conrad Levinson, author of Guerrilla Marketing Excellence, "avoid the use of humor unless it is pertinent to your offering and does not detract from your offer."[3] Marketing does not have to be funny to move people. Especially if you are telling or using an over told joke. It becomes trite, and the customers put up their trickery shield. Your product and/or service, what you say and what you are offering should all have continuity with one another. Rather than being funny it should be convincing to the customer not through laughs but why they should care. Customers are not wondering "Who are you? What is your product or service? When are you open? Where are you located? The reality is that the only real question in the customer's mind is, Why should I care?"[4]

You should always get an outsider's opinion on your marketing. Just because you and everyone that works with and around you like the marketing idea and think it is funny, does not mean your customer will.

The Marketing Professional is an Investment

The marketing profession is not a FP (Fluff Puff) career. It is a serious business discipline. People are not born marketers, it is a discipline that can be learned. But it takes the right mix of talent. Edward S. McKay, author of The Marketing Mystique describes the many ingredients in profiling a master marketer. Here are what I believe the 7 key ingredients are:

1. An unwavering commitment to marketing.
2. An entrepreneurial and a natural innovator.
3. Refined business judgement.
4. A master of the risk/results relationship.
5. A well-rounded understanding and appreciation of the functions of finance, legal, accounting, information technology, administrative services, human resources, sociology, and sales.

6. A combination of analytical and creative abilities to envision new approaches; a right-brain, left-brainer.

7. Soundness of character and the personality to sell ideas, inspire action, and elicit cooperation.

For those of you that are new to the marketing field, it is my sincerest hope that you joined with the notion that it would be hard work rather than a cushy thing to do. Because if it is the latter, you will stick out like a sore thumb at results time in the new millennium. If you want to be a serious marketing professional that adds significant value to an organization, you must be in for the sweat. Those that do will be rewarded with more success than those that do not. Just ask any Olympic Gold Medallist what they did in "their spare time."

The Field Expert

Sergio Zyman, author of The End of Marketing as We Know It, states, "Marketing Professionals are hired for their expertise therefore others with no marketing skills and abilities should not be commenting on or controlling the marketing activities and strategies."[5] If this is too rigid for you, think about this analogy: Would you go to an automobile mechanic to get a tooth pulled? Or better yet, would you challenge a lawyer on a legal evaluation? The same situation applies here "their opinions are valid but only in their field of expertise."[6]

Are scientists popular? Not usually. They can be intense, inquisitive, scrutinizing, and difficult. As a professional marketer you will be all of those things but this is where your talent in tact will play one of its most important roles.

To be successful in marketing you should pay attention to what is going on in the world and how it affects people. Spend time to get to know what affects your customers. The newspaper and CNN are not sufficient mediums to determine trends. You need to create your own marketing experiences by finding out what the trends are and then experience them yourself whenever possible. You will need to pay attention to the stock market, interest rates, trends in restaurants, clothing, voting, politics, economics, fads, and sports.

Chapter 6
Rule #6—Measure Performance

"We can always find time to do it over,
but never the time to do it right in the first
place."

—*Anonymous*

Measuring performance means you are scientifically managing your experiments by documenting your marketing and evaluating progress so you can debrief success. In this chapter we will explore the measurement of the Marketing discipline, discover the 5 T's of Tracking, identify two new disciplines that are paramount to the measurement of marketing; the Cost Per Result analysis and the Payback Axiom, and implement the discipline of measuring the performance of customers interests. The closer you are to the customers pulse the closer you are to measuring results.

Get on the Pulse

In order to measure performance, you need to set up the series of marketing sources identified to generate new customers to your business. These are the sources you will have listed in the Promotion section of your new 7 P's marketing plan. In some cases, this may already be done for you in the software program you use but you must challenge that information. The sources may have been input quite some time ago and therefore not current. Or you may have no choice but to use the standard sources your company has set up. In the later case, you should comply with the set up as required, but be sure to make the inquiry if it can be changed to fit your marketing plan measurement strategy. Once you have the sources set up it is important that you inform every team member of the sources you are using to evaluate the marketing program. It is important that you do not accept "other" or any other vague entry as a valid customer source. If you have multiple ads on the Internet, you will need to distinguish between them in your database. In addition, you should ask the team to be on the look out for new advertising sources used by the competition. This can be best accomplished by briefly and tactfully interviewing the customers. And before you launch the marketing plan you should take the customers pulse. Although marketing is about taking action, in this case you will ask before you act. You may be under pressure to get the plan implemented but you should take the customers pulse first. In some cases, it takes only a day, in others, up to a week. For many, the lack of new customers is the problem. If you have zero customers, then this pre-strategy will not work. But if you have at least 5 weekly customer's (phone or visitor) this strategy will be effective.

Tactfully interview each customer that calls and/or visits. During the sales presentation ask questions about where they searched to find out about you and get to know their interests. This is not accomplished by only asking them what marketing source brought them to you. Your goal is to get into the mind of the customer by asking them questions that will give you buying patterns. Ask them such things as what radio station, mall, restaurants, activities, their last vacation, if they are connected, etc. You should not rattle off a list and do not give them a questionnaire to fill out to save you time from asking. A questionnaire is ineffective because customers will be too tempted to tell you what they think you want to hear. You will get more honest and fresh answers if the customer does not feel as if the information is being recorded. If you show genuine interest to get to know them, you will not only get all the information you need to assist in your marketing strategy, you will likely be rewarded with their business.

Document the responses from the customer interviews. Analyze the information and you will be closer to determining where you should focus your marketing energies.

Get Accurate Data

It is implicit to the measurement of marketing that the measured data you analyze is the actual data. The initial customer contact, in the case of real estate, is the customer card. The customer data that is gathered at the time of their phone call and/or visit is not only a sales tool, it is one of the most cost effective tools in determining future marketing strategies. Despite the customer cards importance and effectiveness, they often get pushed aside. At busy real estate communities, additional factors can be such things as misplaced, ignored, short staffed, and/or the team is in a hurry to close business for the night. They fail to input them into the database, all of which is a common occurrence in the downsized employment force. By the next day, they are forgotten about and with each day it often compounds. As a result, the customer data never gets input into the computer to be measured. Or worst yet, it gets input inaccurately and in most cases, in a catch all tracking category such as "other."

Whenever there is a transfer of information from one place to another there is opportunity for inaccuracies. At any place of business, it is often impossible to take your customer card and immediately input the information into the computer. The longer it takes to get input the greater the opportunity for inaccuracy increases.

For example, you can not say: "Thank You Mr. or Mrs. Customer for all your information but before I can show you this real estate, I have to input your information into my computer right now so it gets reported accurately. I also am concerned that if it gets really busy later, I will not be the one that gets to input it and the person that does might make a mistake or be too lazy to use all your information for our database. And, I might need to leave on time to pick up my kids so I don't get charged $10 a minute for going over and therefore rush out the door before I can input not just your information but all of today's customer information."

In the real world, it takes a significant amount of time to input all the information and that can take you away from the front door to stand meet and greet new customers. Also there is the potential of someone else other than the original collector of the data, who is not directly a part of the sales team and/or a recipient of any commission, input the information. Often they do not take appropriate care and attention to input all the correct information. People have different motivational levels and interests and although we aspire to build teamwork, a person's laziness can get the best of them. This is why the computer is giving you the wrong information. The information is wrong because people made it wrong by being in a hurry, lazy, distracted, or simply by not caring. If you employ the discipline of checking the customer cards against the computer you will find out for yourself how common these inaccuracies are. In the new millennium it is crucial to the success of the marketing effort that the customer data information be input accurately and timely.

Investment in technological means such as a hand held computer and/or kiosks to input information at the point of customer contact is your best advantage in overcoming this obstacle.

The 5 T's of Tracking

Accurately tracking customer data is one of the biggest challenges we face today in implementing the Marketing measurement discipline. I have developed the 5 T's of Tracking to ensure the customer tracking discipline is implemented and reported accurately when technological advances such as hand held computers or kiosks are not available:

1. Train the team on the importance of conducting customer interviews to get buying patterns and to find new advertising source streams.
2. Train the team and develop a strategy on how to complete the customer card with the customer and the process of getting all the customer data in a conversational manner and most importantly "why" we need the information; to ensure successful marketing strategies as a result of measured customer data.
3. Train the team on a strategy to get the customer card data into the computer accurately and on a timely basis.
4. Train the team on teamwork in regards to customer card data computer input for others.
5. Train the team on their shop report and inform them that they will be mystery shopped by someone posing as a customer and their ability to gather the customer card data conversationally and their ability to conduct customer interest interviews will be graded. In addition, inform them they will be graded on the accuracy of customer cards matching the computer database and the marketing source information provided by the mystery shopper.

Perception is who's answering the question

When you begin to analyze your customer data you may be a bit surprised with what it reveals. You may find out for example that only 10 percent of the results are coming from a marketing source that you thought was producing more. This is because many marketing sources get lip service but really do not produce results. Lip service happens when employees communicate a marketing source that they think generates the most customers because it is what they remember in absence of checking the data. Many employees are not aware of the concept of CPR; Cost Per Result discipline. They will usually only speak in terms of what they know and remember. To experience this, conduct a test. Ask any employee what marketing source generates the most customer results and then write it down. Then do an analysis of the marketing sources and see if the source they believe is the one that actually brings the best results. Only 40% of people are right when asked to perform this test. The answer you are given therefore reflects more about who is answering the question rather than the marketing source data itself. The answer you were given was based on their perception. Perception is not reality in this situation and therefore only depends on who's answering the question.

Here is a well-known example of perception: A person enters an unfamiliar market and immediately sees lots of opportunities but the familiar inhabitant's report; "situation hopeless, local natives do not wear shoes." The millennium marketer reports; "situation unlimited, no shoes here, we can get all the market share, send all available shoes."

Perform CPR

The CPR (Cost Per Result) discipline is a measurement tool for the Marketing discipline. You can perform the CPR discipline with these steps:

1. Determine how much customer traffic was generated per marketing source in a given period (usually one month) then determine how many resulted in a sale per marketing source.
2. Determine how many sales resulted in a cancellation for each marketing source.
3. Determine how many sales after cancellations for each marketing source, which becomes your net sales. To calculate this—subtract your cancellations from the gross sales and you will arrive at your net sales number for each source.
4. Determine the cost for each marketing source for the reviewed time period. This can be obtained by reviewing your marketing/advertising invoices.
5. Determine the cost of each generated customer for each marketing source. To calculate this you divide the total cost of the source by the total number of customers from #1.

6. Determine the cost of each net sale per marketing source which becomes your Cost Per Result. To calculate this you divide the total cost of the source by the number of net sales for that source.

For example, a real estate rental property that generated 15 customers from an Internet ad in 30 days, and achieved 8 net sales/results, and the cost of the Internet ad was $95 for the month, you would divide $95 by 8, which is $11.88 (rounded) CPR. You can also calculate the cost per generated customer by applying the same principle but remember the customer result is our measuring stick not how many customers we generated.

You should take action and perform this discipline and analyze the information. Whether it is computer generated or not, get it implemented as soon as possible. Performing the CPR analysis means you are performing marketing science. In order to debrief success you need to track and analyze the customer data. Before you can decide which marketing tactics to use or continue to use, you need to analyze the CPR.

Fish where the fish are

Now that you're CPR certified, it is time to go fishing. If you are achieving a positive result in a specific area, now is not the time to say "if it's not broken don't fix it," and move on. This is because you must challenge your success in order to repeat and improve upon it. An old saying is "fish where the fish are." In this case you will fish where the fish are but with more intensity.

Many believe that by applying intensity to what already brings results is a waste of time, energy, and money. After all if the results are good, let's move on to something else. Wrong. This is because you already found out where your market is, now you need to say more to them. If you are achieving a positive result in a certain area, chances are you have not fully challenged it yet. Since your job in marketing is to manage experiments, you should be willing to take a risk and manage this fishing experiment on your own. Fortunately, you are taking a risk on a source that has already afforded positive results.

It is likely that you will be challenged by naysayers while trying to fish where the fish are because it is considered by many to be radical marketing. The traditional marketers typically do not believe in this tactic. They are not informed about the success of radical marketing tactics that are producing results.

If you are getting positive results from an Internet ad, experiment by upgrading the level of service or investigate into adding another Internet ad source. If you are getting results from a newspaper ad, experiment with a larger ad. This will give you the opportunity to add more newsworthy information potentially increasing the readerships selective perception factor.

A Field Experience…A community had been advertising on a particular Internet site for over 5 months but had not provided any pictures or a virtual tour. Once I became involved, I upgraded the ad with pictures, a virtual tour, and other "design for the mind" tactics. The Cost Per Result for this marketing source was reduced to a CPR of only $13. Although the upgrade presented additional cost, the return on investment more than paid for the upgrade. This positive result was achieved by challenging the existing marketing and giving the self-service customer what they want.

A Field Experience…A community had been advertising in the newspaper with the same ad for over 4 months. When I became involved in the marketing effort at this community I analyzed the customer cards and the computer information and determined the newspaper was generating 25 percent of the communities leases/results. I upgraded the newspaper ad but with just 5 additional lines with targeted words to reach a more vast audience thus achieving selective perception. The leases generated from the newspaper ad increased from 25% to 65% in less than 30 days.

If you are getting positive results from an advertising publication such as in a real estate guide, rental guide, etc., you should consider increasing your advertising. I am a proponent of 2-page ads. The industry jargon for this is called a double truck. In many cases you can utilize the space more efficiently and say more to more people. By saying more you are more likely to strike a chord in someone's mind. They will be more likely to experience selective perception with more information but good graphic design requires that you still leave some white space. That is the challenging part. Your advertising representative should assist you with this. Only after you accomplish the fishing where the fish are tactics should you begin to reach out to un-chartered markets.

A Field Experience…While marketing for a community, I determined one of its most effective sources of customer leases was the rental guides in which we were advertising in the two most predominant publications. One of the guides was producing more leases but in this situation I took a risk and experimented by upgrading the guide that was actually generating the least leases of the two guides. By expanding to a double truck ad and adding floor plans, additional pictures, and more newsworthy information, this guide far exceeded the other guides results. We doubled the generated leased performance. Fishing where the fish are often requires a willingness to take risks and experiment.

What does a Harley, a Virgin, and a Deadhead have to do with marketing?

"A visceral connection to the customer, a long term commitment to the cause, and a willingness to work with and make the best of what's at hand."[1] These are the three lessons discussed by the two authors Sam Hill and Glenn Rifkin, who performed extensive research on the subject of "Radical Marketing." The authors are referring to such radical marketers as Harley Davidson, Virgin Airlines, and the Grateful Dead; among many others as described in their book Radical Marketing.

If you are not familiar with the success of these radicals here is a brief summary on one of them; Harley Davidson. This company, once on the brink of bankruptcy due to fierce competition and quality issues, recreated itself by applying the 3 lessons. Lesson number one stands out most. They had a "visceral connection to the customer."[2] They recognized whom the customer was and said something more and something significant to them. Marketing to the five senses is the goal of any marketer. Harley marketed to the sense of hearing. They transformed the once thought of loud, obnoxious, and burley sound of the engine to a sound that literally makes the heart beat of the passionate Harley customer. Everyone recognizes the sound of a HOG. "For many, the Harley roar is classic noise pollution. But for the Harley lovers, it is a mating call."[3] They accomplished branding. Working towards the sense of identity approach, a brilliant radical marketer came up with the idea to have a club for the few but loyal Harley followers. It was called the Harley Owners Group, or HOG and the HOG membership has its rewards. Owners of a Harley could rent a Harley in any city while travelling. The HOG club created a link to the Harley customer for the struggling company. They fished where the fish were and "a $20 million dollar business in 1988 grew to $100 million by 1996."[4]

Fish for Results

In the real estate field experience I provided, of upgrading advertising where your market is already bringing you results, provides you the opportunity to say something to your customer and more space to do it thus satisfying selective perception. Once the customer purchases from you, your customer retention efforts will have to be significant. In the Harley analogy the customer was already a customer. In the real estate application we are identifying where your typical current customer went to find out about you before they moved in to your community, home, or office space. Once you find out where those places are and capitalize on them you will be catching more fish for fishing where the fish are.

Get on the PA System

In the financial industry, budgets, assumptions, and variance analysis are commonplace. A typical budget consists of revenue and expenses and assumptions for each. Since this book is not about budgeting this budget analogy only includes revenue and expenses. With this budget in place we are asked to perform a variance analysis to explain the positive and negative variances from our assumptions.

Marketers should have to prepare a variance analysis based on the performance of their marketing. I named this discipline The Payback Axiom or PA system. The Payback Axiom is a results oriented, variance-reporting discipline that provides a measurement of the marketing strategy. It should become a requirement, a SOP of every marketing professional. Technology is already bringing this information to the forefront and in real time. Whether performed by technology or the paper way, the Payback Axiom should include the following information (by month and/or by quarter):

1. A list of each marketing source for the business.
2. The monthly budget and actual monthly cost of each marketing source.
3. The budget to actual variance and the percent of variance of each marketing source.
4. The number of net sales per marketing source.
5. The total monthly revenue generated by marketing source. Either use the actual numbers of each rental/sale or determine the average rental/sale amount for the asset as an estimate.
6. The total annual revenue generated by marketing source.
7. The monthly Return on Investment (determined by dividing the marketing source actual cost by the monthly revenue generated).

8. The annual ROI (determined by dividing the marketing source actual cost by the annual revenue generated).
9. A brief narrative for each positive or negative variance.
10. An action plan to improve, invest, and/or advise of course correction where appropriate.

In order to determine the number of net rentals/sales per marketing source you will need to refer to the CPR analysis. In order to determine the total monthly revenue generated you will need to either add all the net rentals/sales monthly amounts together or determine what the businesses average monthly rental/sale amount is and use it for your calculation. Using the same methodology you can calculate the annual revenue generated by multiplying by 12.

Many of you may be thinking "that's nothing new, we look at that stuff and some of us already produce an analysis of this." If that is the case, great. But are you doing it in the timely, results oriented standard and taking action based on the reported data where appropriate? And consistently?

Fortunately, there are software programs that will track these results for you and in real time. "For marketing taking its cues from customer's wants and reactions, the real time tool with the most radical benefits has to do with measurement."[5] This is a good point, but that is the easy part. Analyzing it and completing #10 of the PA; making marketing decisions and taking action on the findings is not only the most challenging part it is one of the most under performed disciplines. Just because technology will provide us with this information does not mean your marketing problems are solved. The new technology that provides us glorified real time marketing reports are a waste of time if they are not used to make decisions and take action in "real time." You may not have real time capabilities now. If not, you are a Migrator. For those that do have it or it is in progress, you are leaders and if the technology is there and used to make decisions and take action, in real time, you will gain the most market share and the most profits.

If you already have a basic measurement of customer data tracking relating to the return on investment, begin analyzing it to make marketing decisions and take immediate action. At least by doing so you are not one of the guilty parties of losing profit. If you are not computerized, you will need to do a lot of old style research and documentation to get all the information that we have reviewed.

Completing number ten of the Payback Axiom is the most challenging and time consuming part. Since it is impossible to be specific, as I do not have your data analysis, I will offer these suggestions before you make any unnecessary course corrections based on your variances.

Marketing is about managing experiments, but in this case change, by way of course corrections, is good. When you make course corrections you are performing marketing science. You should be willing to experiment and take risks. If you find that you have marketing sources that are not generating customers and thus are resulting in a net expense, you should thoroughly investigate why before you make the course correction. In addition is not uncommon to be data rich and information poor. This means you have lots of data but the information may be inaccurate, misleading and/or poor. "Information is not knowledge until we analyze it and understand it. Knowledge is not power until we learn how to use it."[6] Assuming the data input is accurate, you can move on, but if you are at all in doubt of its accuracy, you should perform an audit before you make any course correction.

Once the discipline of the Payback Axiom is implemented, marketing will no longer be viewed as an expense. It will be viewed as an investment. The Payback Axiom is another form of debriefing success. We will correct things that turn out to be wrong and build on things that go right.

Marketers should come to realize that some portions of their advertising will be wasted. The science comes from determining those wasted portions.

Marketing is an implicit function to garner profit in any business. Prove it by debriefing your success by performing the measurement disciplines.

Chapter 7
Rule #7—Problems are Delayed Solutions

"An optimist sees an opportunity in every calamity;
A pessimist sees a calamity, in every opportunity."

—*Anonymous*

In this Chapter we will challenge problems and overcome them with the READY Discipline and reveal the Universal Formula. The READY discipline turns problems into opportunities and transforms those opportunities into results. I have developed a 5-step process that can be used to implement a solution. The Universal Formula identifies and predicts the lease-up, stabilization, and/or recovery time of an under performing real estate asset based on any available historical data for the community and/or market. Its application is truly universal and applicable to many other industries. It is a mathematically proven, scientific formula, that when applied and strategized properly, will produce results. No matter what industry you are in, you will benefit from the Universal Formula. Since the problem is not always the issue presented we will also discuss a professional discipline of discovering the underlying problems and the skill of exposing them with tact.

Get READY

The READY discipline is a formula that turns problems into opportunities and transforms those opportunities into results. You must be willing to challenge all the problems no matter how significant or insignificant they may appear. In every problem there is a unique opportunity waiting to be discovered, waiting to bring results. I have a 5-step process that can be used to implement the solution. I call it the READY discipline.

1. Recognize
2. Evaluate
3. Action
4. Dedication
5. Yes

1. **Recognize** there are problems and problems are delayed solutions. Challenge everything. Make a list of all the problems you have with your marketing. Maybe the problem is you do not have any. Discuss why. Make a list of objections and excuses.

2. **Evaluate** each one. Many of the problems listed in #1 are the actual solution to the others. You will only discover them if you approach this with an open mind and in terms of the customer and not yourself. Put yourself in their shoes and evaluate each problem as if you were the customer. One of the biggest mistakes we make in marketing is we decide what we want or would want and forget that it does not matter what we want.

3. **Action**, now you have your list. You now should decide which opportunities you are going to implement and take action on. Step 3 is not just about writing or talking about what you plan to implement, it is about taking action; meaning the physical action of doing it, or delegating it to someone to do it and then ensuring that they do it.

4. **Dedication,** be dedicated to the cause and do not give up. While taking action, you may encounter the naysayers of the world. The naysayer is someone who sees your action as a threat and will try to convince you that you are wasting time on a problem. This is where you interject with

your enthusiasm to the cause. You will be practicing radical marketing lesson #2, "a long term commitment to the cause."[1] Naysayers can be difficult creatures and will often try to stifle your enthusiasm. Do not listen to the naysayers. They are only trying to stop you from getting to step five, which is where the true fun and profit begins.

5. **Yes**, the results are in and it is a victory. You recognized, evaluated, took action, were dedicated, and yes, the results are victorious. You have now achieved the READY discipline and it has rewards! You will be paid back with the positive results of your achievements. Nobody can argue with results, especially the naysayers. Who, by the way, will be either sulking in the corner, taking credit for the results, or say they knew you could do it the whole time. You should always keep track of these achievements.

The Universal Formula
What is the secret? Many people are curious about how I achieve Marketing results. The answer is, there is no secret. But there is a universal formula to identify and predict the lease-up, stabilization, and/or recovery time of a real estate asset based on historical data for the community and/or market. Regardless of the situation and the current asset, this formula works. It is not new, it is not a secret, it is not magical, it is not art, and it is not mine. It is a mathematical, scientific formula that is used and applicable in many other industries; it has a proven track record. The Universal Formula has many names but the underlying formula is the same for all. And, once it's formulated and the Playbook is implemented, results will follow.

Scientific interpretation strives for clarity and proof, "such proof of understanding will be either of rational, i.e., logical or mathematical, or of an emotionally empathic, artistic appreciative character."[2] Since the Universal Formula's interpretation is logical, mathematical, emotional, and of artistic character, it should get the attention of all marketers.

The Universal Formula is fundamentally sound and should be included as a primary function of the Marketing discipline; the solicitation of new customers. However, keep in mind that in sociology, according to Max Weber, author of Basic Concepts in Sociology, averages can be "formulated with greater precision only where it is a matter of qualitatively equal in behavior but differing merely in degrees."[3] Which means that if you are using industry averages to make your average determinations, such as in a lease-up/sales situation with no historical data available, it is important to evaluate the employees closing ratio (sales) averages from the past. But the employees in which you compare should have averages that differ only slightly or you will have disparity in results.

Many times, examples are not grounded in a specific discipline and therefore is too generalized. Although this example is specific to real estate, you can rework it to fit your Marketing strategy.

The Formula
V+N+FO+S=RN (Vacants + Notices + Fall Out + Skips = Rentals Needed)

RN ÷ CACR = CT (Rentals Needed ÷ Current Average Closing Ratio = Customer Traffic)

CACT x CACR = CRA (Current Average Customer Traffic x Current Average Closing Ratio = Current Rentals Achieved)

CRA – RN = NRN (Current Rentals Achieved–Rentals Needed = New Rentals Needed)

Or…Number of Vacants Not Rented + Number of Notices Not Rented + Number of "Additional Notices/Fall-out" (this is based on your historical turnover rate) + Estimated Skips = Rentals Needed.

Then you take the Rental Needed and divide it by the Current Average Closing Ratio to determine how much Customer Traffic you need to generate to achieve the Rentals Needed.

Then you take the Current Average Customer Traffic (monthly) x Current Average Closing Ratio (monthly) = Current Rentals Achieved.

Then you take the Current Rental Achieved and subtract (-) it from the Rentals Needed to determine how many additional rentals you need to achieve the total New Rentals Needed.

How to Determine Fall-Out: One of the most common reasons for not attaining a rental goal in the recovery time frame set is because the goal was not set scientifically and realistically. You must factor in the "fall-out" that will happen as a result of your intensity with your current customers. Fall-Out is the terminology for the additional notices you will receive while your marketing plan is in action based on historical customer turnover data. A goal that only factors in current vacancies, current notices, and potential skips, is unrealistic because there is always going to be fall-out. And since your time frame for recovery factors in how much customer traffic you need to achieve the rental goal, you will fall short in customer traffic thus falling short in rentals by not having the fall-out notices covered while your plan is underway. You will get additional notices based on your average turnover rate and by forcing current customers to make a decision even if it's to move out.

For instance if you have a historical turnover rate of 65% each month, and you have received 5 notices out of the 26 expirations for that month, chances are you will get another 12 notices from that set of expirations. At least by factoring the "fall-out" into your rental goal, you will be focussed on the additional customer traffic needed in order to fill their places rather than scrambling later for additional customer traffic when you realize you have fallen short of your goal.

An example is this: You have 30 expirations for the month. 5 have already given notice leaving 25 more exposed to potentially give notice. Once you apply renewal intensity with the 25 people that have not made a move-out or renewal decision yet, you have to expect that you will get additional notices from them. 30 expirations in a month (based on a 65% turnover rate) is going to result in 20 potential move-out notices. If you have already received 5 notices, you need to add 15 to your rental goal to cover the additional potential fall-out. If your goal time frame is 30 days, you will need to factor in at least 2 months of expirations; and the potential fall-out. Count any notices already received and then calculate the fall-out for each month and then add it to your rental goal.

The Universal Formula (Sample Case Study)

The following is a sample case study on a community to further demonstrate this activity.

Case Study:

Happy Acres Apartments is a 360-unit rental community located in a "soft market." Current Occupancy is 91% or 328 occupied units. Current Percent Leased is 89% or 321 units currently leased. There is a total of 39 units exposed or "available" to rent. 20 of the 39 available units to rent are vacant and the remaining 19 are on notice to vacate. The Owner has given a time frame for Recovery of 30 days in which to achieve 100% occupancy. The current average turnover rate is 65%. It's the first of March. Your 19 notices are from March and April lease expirations. The total expirations for March is 22; 10 of which have already given notice. Based on 65% turnover each month we must anticipate an additional 4 notices from March as "Fall-Out." The total expirations for April is 24; 9 of which have already given notice. Using the same methodology we must anticipate an additional 7 notices from April as "Fall-Out."

*The total Percent Leased is determined by the total number of leased occupied units, vacant units that are rented, and notices that are already rented/assigned. The surplus of units is considered the potential exposure to vacancy (39).

Using the information above, we can begin completing the universal formula and determine the marketing strategy.

Goal is 100% or 360 units Occupied and Pre-Leased.

Number of Vacants not rented: 20

+ Number of Notices not rented: 19

+ Fall-Out/Additional Notices: 11 (March notices so far is 10; expect 4 more, April notices is 9; expect 7 more)

+ Skips: 0

= Rental Needed: 50

Rentals Needed (50) ÷ Current Average Closing Ratio (25%) = Customer Traffic needed to achieve Rentals Needed: 200.

Current Average Customer Traffic (monthly) (100) x Current Average Closing Ratio (monthly) (25%) = Current Rental Achieved: 25

Current Rentals Achieved (25) – Rentals Needed: (50) = New Rentals Needed: 25.

The Universal Formula Reality Check:

In order to determine/predict the time frame for recovery, you need to take a reality check. If the number of Rentals Needed (50) is higher than the Current Rentals Achieved (25) then you must consider these options:

1. Increase Customer Traffic to the number of Customer Traffic needed to achieve the additional New Rentals Needed. How much more would customer traffic have to be increased if closing ratio's remained the

same? Rentals Needed (50) ÷ Current Average Closing Ratio (25%) = 200 Total Customer Traffic – Current Average Customer Traffic = 100 extra customer traffic needed.

2. Increase Closing Ratios by the percent needed to meet the Current Average Customer Traffic amount in order to achieve the Rentals Needed thus not needing to increase customer traffic. How much more would closing ratio's have to increase if traffic remained the same? Rentals Needed (50) ÷ Current Average Customer Traffic (100) = 50% New Closing Ratio.

Next determine "upside" and "downside" time frame for recovery based on options 1 and 2 by themselves and also on a combination of 1 and 2 with variables.

The upside to #1 is by generating 100 more customer traffic/or 25 more customer traffic per week, the goal of 50 rentals would be achieved in 30 days. This is attainable by implementing the "Playbook." The down-side is you may not be adequately staffed to handle the 100 new customer traffic. You should consider hiring additional help if you plan to take this route.

The upside to #2 is by increasing closing ratio's from 25% to 50% you do not have to generate any more customer traffic thus not needing to hire any additional help. This strategy should include a comprehensive leasing/sales skills refresher class for all leasing staff. The downside is the lack of time and possible resources to accomplish this. Time is of the essence and if they are in training, they are not leasing units. Also if the 50% closing ratio is not consistently achieved, the goal will not be met in the Owners 30-day time frame.

If you determine or set the goals based on current customer traffic and closing ratio's remaining the same, then you can predict the time frame for recovery with a degree of accuracy. This is based on the amount of time it will take you to generate the total Customer Traffic to achieve the Rentals Needed. At Happy Acres, if we sat idly and did nothing, we would only achieve 25 of the 50 needed rentals in the Owners time frame; thus resulting in an unhappy Owner. Rather it is wise to set your objectives to increase customer traffic and increase closing ratio's simultaneously thus shrinking the time frame for recovery.

The upside to combining number 1 and 2 is a strategy that requires the staff to increase customer traffic through Marketing and improve closing ratio's simultaneously. It is usually the most cost-effective route to take.

Action: Based on all the available information in this case study and this Playbook, I am prepared to recommend the following course of action for Happy Acres:

Action Goals and Objectives:

1. Generate a minimum of 34 qualified customer traffic per week and achieve 13 net leases per week. The last 4 Weeks indicate a total of 100 customer traffic or an average of 25 customer traffic per week. We need to increase this to 34 customer traffic per week. The customer traffic goal is to generate 35-36 new customer traffic in 30 days. We can achieve this by implementing the "Playbook."

2. The goal is to achieve a minimum of 50 net leases in 30 days. The last 4 weeks indicate a total of 25 leases. We only need 25 more leases than our normal monthly historical performance.

Fall-Out calculation: Based on our current vacants and current notices to vacate, so far our Rentals Needed are 39 units needed in order to get to 100% leased and occupied. But based on a historical 65% retention rate we must anticipate a potential of 4 more Fall-Out notices from March (month) expirations and 7 more Fall-Out from April (month) expirations which is a total of 11 Fall-Out. This is what revised our Rentals Needed to 50.

1. Achieve and maintain closing ratios of at the minimum 37%. The last 4 weeks indicate a closing ratio of 25%. The current performance is too low and should be improved by 12% to 37%. Remember that a higher closing ratio results in less customer traffic needed to be generated to get the same results. If we increase our closing ratio to 37% we only need to generate 35-36 new customer traffic in 30 days. This is attainable with improved leasing skills and increased marketing. We will conduct a comprehensive leasing refresher course; date to be determined with the Manager. Keep in mind, if you remain at 25% closing ratios; you must generate the 100 additional customer traffic in order to meet the time frame for recovery.

2. Happy Acres is to reach an occupancy rate of 100% by March 31.

Once you have completed the Universal Formula and implemented this Playbook, unprecedented results will follow.

The Universal Formula Worksheet
The following is a blank Universal Formula Worksheet for your use in completing this exercise on your own.

Goal is ____% or ___ units Occupied and Pre-Leased.

Number of Vacants not rented: ___

+ Number of Notices not rented: ___

+ Fall-Out/Additional Notices: ___ (_____ (month) notices is ___; expect ___ more, _____ (month) notices is ___; expect ___ more)

+ Skips: __

= Rental Needed: ___

Rentals Needed (__) ÷ Current Average Closing Ratio (__%) = Customer Traffic needed to achieve Rentals Needed: ___.

Current Average Customer Traffic (monthly) (___) x Current Average Closing Ratio (monthly) (__%) = Current Rental Achieved: ___

Current Rentals Achieved (___) – Rentals Needed: (__) = New Rentals Needed: ___.

The Universal Formula Reality Check:

In order to determine/predict the time frame for recovery, you need to take a reality check. If the number of Rentals Needed (__) is higher than the Current Rentals Achieved (__) then you must consider these options:

1. Increase Customer Traffic to the number of Customer Traffic needed to achieve the additional New Rentals Needed. How much more would customer traffic have to be increased if closing ratios remained the same? Rentals Needed (__) ÷ Current Average Closing Ratio (__%) = ___ Total Customer Traffic – Current Average Customer Traffic = ___ extra customer traffic needed.

2. Increase Closing Ratio's by the percent needed to meet the Current Average Customer Traffic amount in order to achieve the Rentals Needed thus not needing to increase customer traffic. How much more would closing ratio's have to increase if traffic remained the same? Rentals Needed (__) ÷ Current Average Customer Traffic (___) = ___% New Closing Ratio.

Next determine "upside" and "downside" time frame for recovery based on options 1 and 2 by themselves and also on a combination of 1 and 2 with variables.

The upside to #1 is by generating ___ more customer traffic/or ___ more customer traffic per week, the goal of ___ rentals would be achieved in ___ days. This is attainable by implementing the "Playbook." The downside is you may not be adequately staffed to handle the ___ new customer traffic. You should consider hiring additional help if you plan to take this route.

The upside to #2 is by increasing closing ratio's from ___% to ___%, you do not have to generate any more customer traffic thus not needing to hire any additional help. This strategy should include a comprehensive leasing/sales skills refresher class for all leasing staff. The downside is the lack of time and possible resources to accomplish this. Time is of the essence and if they are in training, they are not leasing units. Also if the ___% closing is not consistently achieved, the goal will not be met in the Owners ___ days time frame.

If you determine or set the goals based on current customer traffic and closing ratio's remaining the same, then you can predict the time frame for recovery with a degree of accuracy. This is based on the amount of time it will take you to generate the total Customer Traffic to achieve the Rentals Needed. At _____(name of community) if we continue at status quo, we would only achieve ___ of the ___ needed rentals in the Owners time frame; thus resulting in an unhappy Owner. Rather it is wise to set your objectives to increase customer traffic and increase closing ratio's simultaneously thus shrinking the time frame for recovery.

The upside to combining number 1 and 2 is a strategy that requires the staff to increase customer traffic through Marketing and improve closing ratios simultaneously. It is usually the most cost-effective route to take.

Action: Based on all the available information in this case study and this "Playbook." I am prepared to recommend the following course of action for _____(name of community:)

Action Goals and Objectives:

1. Generate a minimum of ___ qualified traffic per week and achieve ___ net leases per week. The last 4 weeks indicate a total of ___

customer traffic or an average of ___ customer traffic per week. We need to increase this to ___ customer traffic per week. The traffic goal is to generate___ new customer traffic in ___ days. We can achieve this by implementing the "Playbook."

2. The goal is to achieve a minimum of ___ net leases in ___ days. The last 4 weeks indicate a total of ___ leases. We only need ___ more leases than our normal monthly historical performance.

Fall-Out calculation: Based on our current vacants and notices to vacate, so far our Rentals Needed are ___ units needed in order to get to ___% leased and occupied. But based on a historical ___% turnover rate we must anticipate a potential of _____ more Fall-Out notices from _____ (month) expirations and ___ more Fall-Out from _____ (month) expirations which is a total of ___ Fall-Out. This is what revised our Rentals Needed to ____.

1. Achieve and maintain closing ratios of at the minimum ___%. The last 4 weeks indicate a closing ratio of ___%. The current performance is too low and should be improved by ___% to ___%. Remember that higher closing ratio results in less customer traffic needed to be generated to get the same results. If we increase our closing ratio to ___% we only need to generate ____ new customer traffic in ____ days. This is attainable with improved leasing skills and increased marketing. We will conduct a comprehensive leasing refresher course; date to be determined with Community Manager. Keep in mind, if remain at ___ closing ratios; you must generate the ____ additional customer traffic in order to meet the time frame for recovery.

2. _____is to reach an occupancy rate of ___% by _____ (date.)

The problem is not always the issue presented

As a marketer you will have internal and external customers whom rely on you for your level of expertise. The following scenario is a common occurrence between marketers and their customers, it is described by Paul Postma, author of The New Marketing Era. "In consultative situations in which we are involved as marketing professionals, messy thinking can be recognized all too easily especially regarding critical strategic problems for which people ask our opionions."[4] When the internal or external customer is interested in marketing advice, it is important to realize the real problem is not the issue that is usually presented by the customer. The customer typically thinks in solutions and presents the problem in terms of a pre-determined solution and then asks the marketing professional to comment. It is a learned skill of the marketing professional to discover the underlying actual problem because the customer who has a vested interest often distorts the actual problem. The customer's fear of failure or exposure to accountability to the actual problem creates defensiveness and a survival mechanism can get triggered, discrediting the marketing professional's analysis. Knowing this, it is a challenge for the marketing professional to expose those distorted views and communicate the final concrete solution. The marketing professional can accomplish this in such a manner that the customer with the vested interest in the findings and outcome becomes mentally transformed from a distorter with a vested interest to a co-creator of the final concrete solution whether they actually participated in it or not. This type of behavioral science in terms of the marketing professionals' communication with the customer is a learned discipline requiring the ability to listen carefully and patiently and should always be approached with tact.

No Agendas

The message to the marketer is, there is no place for an agenda in the marketing arena. As a hired consultant performing in the area of your expertise, exposing faults and shortcomings of a particular business or another person is unprofessional conduct. You should be willing to take responsibility, accountability, and exercise tact in all communications.

For example: If a marketer is involved with a business and performs a marketing audit of activities and finds the business is not following guidelines or have failed to implement their marketing, it is unproductive to point fingers and find fault. Rather, the marketing professional should utilize their time to create a solution and take immediate action to correct in a positive and coaching manner with the employees. While doing so it is equally important to convey a sense of urgency and to set the expectation level for the future.

As a marketing professional, it is your responsibility that the teams you support implement the programs and are doing them correctly. Take immediate responsibility, document the findings in the most positive manner possible, attach a solution and an action plan for each shortcoming and assist in the recovery effort.

Chapter 8
Rule #8—You Must be Willing to Sweat

"Genius is 99% perspiration and 1% inspiration."

—*Thomas Edison*

Marketing is a sweat activity. The Least Effort Principle: "in theories of psychology, this principle states that given certain possibilities for action, an organism will select the one requiring the least effort."[1] Since marketing is an effort this is why the marketing is not getting done.

Marketing is not an optional activity. Any company that wants to grow and produce profits must market. If you ignore the importance of marketing and sit idly, your competition will market for you. Since positioning is a two-way street you need to position yourself before the competition does it for you.

The customers changed the rules

In the past decade many marketers have marketed with the concept of letting the direct competition do the marketing for them. The concept is to endorse your direct competitions advertising and marketing efforts because they are doing all the work and spending their money to generate customers. If you shared the street with them or are nearby you would benefit from their customer traffic by mere proximity to their location. This tactic may have been successful in some markets; however, it will not be as successful in the millennium. If you continually leave it up to your competition to market for you, be prepared to be repositioned because the customers have changed the rules.

The customer has become time conscious. They do not have the luxury of time to drive into your business parking lot just because they saw you inadvertently while they were "shopping" around. They are too informed for that. They are on real time schedule and you are not on it. Marketing professionals should challenge all drive by customer traffic. Especially since it is a fact, customer traffic is not tracked properly yet and drive-by is receiving way too much of the attention. To test and challenge this, simply implement the customer interview discipline as discussed in Chapter Six to determine if drive-by is the actual and/original motivational source that brought the customer to you. If you took a survey of how many sales you made off another companies advertising, the results would likely prove minimal. If you are the exception and this tactic is still working for you, by all means continue. For the majority, rethink this strategy because the customer has changed the rules.

Take some R&R

Not rest and relaxation, this is the sweat chapter! The R&R is a real time rapid response. The more rapidly you respond to the opportunities the closer you are to the other R&R. All too often, opportunities are missed because the response is not rapid enough. Customers want and demand a rapid response. If they do not get it they lose interest or worse yet, they buy from another rapid marketer. One of the first things people used to do when they got home was to open the postal mail. People still do but not as many as before. Because, "You've Got Mail," and it's not snail mail. Snail mail is slow. Electronic cards by e-mail is fast. By responding online to a customer request for information you will gain the most market share. By following up via online you will stay connected to that customer and in real time.

Technology is not the only medium in which to be a rapid response marketer. The most valuable and yet underestimated customers are the ones who solicit your company. This is commonly known and referred to as a request for information. These unsolicited customers are found gold. When you receive their request for information it should not be sent snail mail. Snail mail is guaranteed to arrive after the customer has already given their business to someone else. Millennium customers want it airborne, online and/or overnight. Why are these customers found gold? Because if the customer buys, and it is likely they will, if their request is handled Airborne or online, it results in a CPR of under $10 in most cases; a marketers low cost operating dream.

The message an overnight express package delivers to the customer is that they are important and valued. They will feel wanted and they will recognize you as a market leader and will want to buy from you. Not only will your materials arrive before everyone elses, it is more likely that your materials will be the only ones they receive. Get an express mail account for your team and set a budget for them to utilize it.

A Field Experience…In 15 years of making requests for information from companies, including my competition, I have received less than 10 brochures of information. Recently, I was reviewing one of the rental guides that had a special request for information insert in the book with 7 communities in the ad. I completed the card requesting information from all and only received 2 brochures out of the 7 requested. Of the 2, one included my name and a personal note, while the other was a form letter absent of my specific requests or an invitation to visit.

The companies that provide the most information, in the most cost-effective outlets, rapidly, and with personalization, will win the most market share. You will also keep them by feeding them more information. By more information I do not mean massive information but rather distilling from the input the information that has the highest predictable value to the customers thus triggering their selective perception.

8 underestimated tools by non-guerrilla's

The following are examples of 8 underestimated, underused, and over-looked marketing tactics by non-guerrillas. Mainstream marketers and companies may not be employing these tools because they are not considered "new" and they may be too focussed on the quick fix; the flavor of the week to solve their marketing problems when such a flavor simply does not exist. Whether you are in real estate or not, it is unproductive to think up new marketing flavors when you have yet to challenge and then achieve excellence in these 8 tools.

When evaluating these tools and determining their use, keep in mind that there is a huge difference between simply implementing them and implementing them with excellence. If you have not yet implemented them with excellence (using the cover to cover concepts outlined in this book) then you have never really implemented them and they should be considered "brand new."

1. Customer Cards
2. Newsletter and Newsletter Brochures
3. A Comparison Analysis
4. Direct Mail Marketing
5. Testimonials
6. Flyers
7. On hold Advertising
8. Internet Adverting/Web site

Customer Cards—Once of the most underestimated and underused marketing tactics is your customer cards. Even if you are being assured that the customer cards are being maximized, the only way to know is to check for yourself. Checking is a sweat activity but it is crucial if you plan to measure marketing's effectiveness. Many focus on generating new customers to solve the marketing problem when they already have an archive of new potential customers. Therefore the place to look first is in the archive of current customer cards. They have not just been under marketed by you but also by your competition. Going through the archive of customer cards and designing a campaign to get them back in the door is a sweat activity. Do the sweat and market with this archive of customers and you will get results.

Newsletters and Newsletter Brochures—The newsletter is another one of the most underestimated and underused marketing tools. Contributing to the problem as it pertains to real estate is that many actually believe it is a customer retention tool and therefore only for the current customers. When believed as such, it is tempting not to utilize them because they are not viewed as paying a direct return. When this tool hit the real estate industry in the early 1990's many were convinced it was a customer retention tactic mainly because it was marketed as such by the pioneering companies of this product. Its value and effectiveness is demonstrated when it is implemented as part of the Marketing discipline; the solicitation of new customers. The newsletter affords the solicited customers hidden need to be a nosey busy body; I call the NB Factor.

Studies have shown that people may not read your brochure, prospectus, or your ads, but they will read a 4-color 4-page newsletter. It satisfies their insatiable curiosity and the hidden need to do so. People are nosey by nature and want access to newsworthy information. So satisfy their curiosity by putting together an upbeat and informative newsletter that serves a dual purpose.

One of the most effective marketing tools is the use of a newsletter brochure. The inside pages can serve as your floor plan display or product and/or service information, and the front and back cover for area information, a map, directions, and an area to place an address for direct mailing. It is one of the least expensive, color quality brochure ideas you can use to solicit new customers.

Since the new "experience economy" is not just about goods and services but rather about staging experiences, marketers have much to gain by staging experiences for their potential customers. Although it may appear insignificant in the grand scheme of becoming an "experience economy," the portrayal of such in a newsworthy medium, such as a newsletter or newsletter brochure, attracts the attention of millennium customers in search of an experience offering.

According to C. Britt Beemer, author of Predatory Marketing, "At a National Center for the 79th Annual DMA (Direct Mailing Association) conference in New Orleans, October 1996; 16 successful new loyalty marketing programs were introduced."[2] It is interesting to note that 8 out of 16 of these programs were newsletters.

The dual purpose of the newsletter is first to serve as a newsworthy brochure of the companies experience factor and second, to serve the current customers by informing them of important dates, additional product and/or service offerings, etc. You should constantly be adding services for your current customers. Communicating those "value added" services in the newsletter is another form of customer retention with a twist on the NB Factor.

A Comparison Analysis—A comparison analysis of your product and/or service versus the competition is an excellent marketing tool. It should be included as part of your collateral package. A professionally printed comparison will receive more credibility than an overused copy on standard copy paper. Although it may be nice to have such a medium on display in the sales area, it is not mobile therefore the customer will not have the opportunity to analyze it at their convenience. The two mediums will have a much greater impact when used in conjunction. One without the other just decreases its effectiveness.

Unfortunately this tool has already bored many marketers. It is implicit to remember that the marketing is not there to entertain or move you. Too many marketers are guilty of marketing for themselves and not for the customers. Furthermore, no matter how tempting, it is not wise to use any type of negative advertising about your competition. Negative ads or referencing do not build customer patronage or loyalty. Negative ads irritate customers who do not want to be associated with mud throwers. Set up your comparative analysis in a factual manner and refrain from throwing mud on the competition to demonstrate your superior offerings. Positive comparative advertising affords benefits such as "it helps you control the dialogue in the market by defining the standards for judgement; and it narrows the position of your competition to an area where it is weaker than you are."[3]

Direct Mail Marketing—If you have tried direct mailing in the past and it was unsuccessful, chances are it was because it wasn't "designed for mind," or part of a measurement discipline, and/or the wrong audience was targeted because direct mail marketing, when properly used, can achieve significant results. In order for direct mailing to be a success you must clearly define who will be the recipient of the mailing. You may choose to do a direct mail brochure, postcard, or flyer to a select group as an experiment. This can be accomplished by purchasing address labels from a direct mailing company that holds a database of them. It is essential that you communicate to the direct mail company that your current customers are not to receive the mailing. In real estate, we typically go by a courier route, but it is likely that your current customers are located in that route. Pay the extra cost to have your current customers addresses pulled to keep your customers from receiving the "solicitation of new customers" mailing. Many real estate marketers are turned off to direct mailers, often due to mistakes made such as the direct mailer being sent to their own customers resulting in a marketing disaster. To avoid this, it is the marketers responsibility to clearly communicate this to the direct mail company and ensure the current customer base is not part of the zip code, route, or otherwise.

In real estate, a very effective direct mailing tactic is to target what I call the "step up" communities in your area. These are the communities that are not direct competition, but are close in location with a rental base within $80-100 of yours (this is usually the effective threshold, but be willing to experiment). Current residents of these communities may be in a position to "step up" their lifestyle as a result of a raise, promotion, and/or by having saved money as a result of living at a lesser expensive community. The American Dream is not necessarily to buy a home and includes the desire to move up the "lifestyle" ladder. This is in effect a means of segmentation marketing. Attitude, values, income, and lifestyle are all segments and if marketed to properly, will result in profits. The same principle applies to commercial real estate. You can target a "step up" group of office parks for instance to reach a business audience that may be in expansion mode and/or in selective perception.

If you design a direct mailer yourself and utilize bulk mail, it can be one of the most cost-effective ways to do mass marketing. Those challenged by their marketing budgets have much to gain by setting up a bulk mail account. Do not let unsuccessful direct mail experiences of the past keep you from this great marketing tactic. And every time you do a direct mailing no matter who you are targeting, you will always reach a new audience. Even the same person who may not have paid it attention in the past may now be in "selective perception."

A Field Experience...One of the many positive experiences I have with direct mailing comes from a community that was faced with an overwhelming amount of move-out notices due to home purchases when the interest rates dropped to an all time low in recent times. I decided to choose 3 "step up" communities in the area and 3 communities that were our direct competition and direct mail them. A tracking mechanism was used so I could determine which of the dual mailing would get the best results. We achieved 8 leases from the 3 step up communities' mailer and only 2 leases from the direct competition mailer. The total cost of the dual marketing mailer was $1,500. The CPR was only $150. The industry average CPR is approximately $175. These 10 leases and the remaining leases derived from the rest of the playbook marketing we had in place solved our exposure to vacancy and the community recovered in less than 30 days.

Every time you use a direct mailing it is a learning experience. "The more you use it and learn the better it performs if you do your homework."[4]

Direct mailing is also effective when used to mail an offer to an archive of past customer cards, Chamber of Commerce listings, business listings, and customized mailing lists that match your demographic profile and are likely to be in "selective perception" mode. A direct mailer might be just what you need to get your marketing jumpstarted.

Testimonials—Kevin Kelly, author of The New Rules for the New Economy says, "follow the free." You should take advantage of every opportunity to give a free sampling of your product and/or service whenever possible. America Online (AOL) was the master at achieving outstanding results as a result of this strategy. In every industry, the freest form of a product and/or service sampling is from testimonials. They are one of the most effective, no cost, marketing tools available. Marketers should always have testimonials on hand to include with marketing packages for networking in the business community and include such quotes from satisfied customers in their advertising. When customers see testimonials, especially from people they relate to, they will gain confidence in you. The best way to obtain testimonials is to ask your satisfied customers to write them and/or offer to write it for them and then have them sign it. This allows you to "control" the content. Testimonials are more believable than your ads so utilize them as often as possible.

Flyers—Flyers are inexpensive and effective. They are also known as circulars. They can be handed out at street corners, placed on cars, in businesses, restaurants, bulletin boards, schools, posted as signs on poles, break rooms of employers, etc. The primary function of the flyer is to promote an offer and create a sense of urgency to buy now. The use of colored paper is effective but make sure the print is legible. Full color is also effective but for this mass distribution tactic it is cost prohibitive. For a quick reference on designing an effective flyer, review Chapter Three: Design for the Mind to ensure its mindful effectiveness. A new and/or recovering business should be distributing a minimum of 1,000-2,000 flyers in their market place per week for maximum results. The best way to facilitate this process is by "shoe leather marketing."

On hold Advertising—No matter what business you call, it is likely that you will be placed on hold. There are different schools of thought and philosophies about on hold advertising. Some believe it is unnecessary as they never need to put people on hold or they are concerned it will be used irresponsibly. The more modern school of thought is the inevitable, callers get placed on hold and when they do you need to be entertaining them or providing them with information. As millennium marketers we will accomplish both. Many marketers do not realize radio music is licensed, and therefore illegal to broadcast unless purchased, not to mention the fact that it is not a good idea since your customers may get to hear a competitors advertisement on the radio while they are on hold waiting for you. On hold advertising is a great marketing tool and it is cost effective. It is suggested that you participate in writing the script and choosing the music to ensure the on hold message is consistent with the overall marketing theme of your business. And don't forget to have your web address and/or toll-free number recited in your message for time-starved customers.

Internet Advertising/Web site—The Internet is the fastest growing media of all time. The Internet is another way to provide customer service but with the new paradigm shift to self-service. By being on the net, you will be available to your customers convenience. Advertising your company on the Internet and providing them with a way to do business with you 24/7 is a profitable business strategy. It will also provide you with the lowest possible "per customer business transaction" cost. If you already have an Internet ad or web site, you should "shop" yourself just to see how "easy" or *"uneasy"* it is to do business with your company.

Take a Fresh Look

There are many underestimated, underused, and overlooked marketing tools and tactics that marketers disregard because of either the sweat factor or their boredom factor. You should be taking a fresh look at all your previous marketing to determine if it should be considered "brand new" again and utilized in the manner in which this Playbook demonstrates even if it involves sweat. Discounting your product and/or services by way of a sale or concession in lieu of using proven marketing "sweat" tools is not good business and will likely cause you to go "out of business." In the new millennium you must be willing to sweat.

Chapter 9
Rule # 9—If You Market, They Will Come

"Things may come to those who wait,
but only the things left by those who hustle."
—*Abraham Lincoln*

It is a fact, you will improve your business if you market. In this chapter we will expose the two most common excuses used that is applicable to all businesses that compete on "location," and then challenge you to overcome them. We will also discuss competition strategies and the importance of building marketing relationships by building a bi-lateral business referral network.

The Soft Market Solution

Excuse number one is a soft market. What if business is slow, sales are down and many begin to blame the market conditions? A soft market is defined as a market that may be overbuilt (too much supply and not enough demand) in decline, or economically unbalanced.

Rule #9 "If you market, they will come," is implicit to winning market share in a soft market. It is about getting out and doing your marketing. In the real estate multi-family and commercial industry, it is about putting heads on beds and derrieres at desks. This can be accomplished in any market, even a soft market.

Soft market; so what! Just because you are stuck in a soft market does not mean you have to stay stuck forever. Make the soft market the other guy's problem; meaning your competition's problem. Marketing will fix any soft market issue. A soft market is not a legitimate excuse to avoid marketing. A solution-oriented marketing professional can solve any soft market issue. We can solve it because we are willing to sweat and the competition is not.

Overcoming a soft market can be achieved by doing such things as a grand opening, grand reopening, or an open house. According to research by C. Britt Beemer, author of Predatory Marketing and founder & CEO of America's Research Group, "94% of people believe a grand opening sale is legitimate."[1] Research also reveals that a successful grand opening or open house can create a positive image for up to 7 years. To create a successful grand opening or open house it will require significant planning and precise execution. Businesses that should consider a grand opening are ones that are brand new or just completed a renovation, rehabilitation, or expansion project. C. Britt Beemers research study also revealed a grand re-opening or open house "can generate 50-60% of what an original grand opening can"[2] and therefore still produces significant results. Real estate should consider a grand re-opening or open house anytime they are faced with a repositioning of an asset due to significant price increases thus forcing out some of the current customers or a situation where it has been "on the market" for a period of time. Those with no prior event planning experience should consult the advice of a consultant and/or event planner. Brainstorm and work out the details so you know what to expect in the execution aspect. Designing the marketing and planning a theme will take time but with a proper game plan and acknowledgement of details, it will be easier and more successful as a result.

A Field Experience…During an intense occupancy recovery in a soft market we were faced with a second lease-up as a result of forcing out current residents that were leased to with high new construction concessions and a market rent increase of up to 15% during the first year. Faced with stiff competition and a need to change the current profile, marketing had to hit the ground running and sweat for every gained percent in occupancy. Several strategies such as increased advertising, flyers, marketing to businesses, etc. were implemented but the home run came from adding the open house to the marketing menu. We promoted it by setting up a model, and inviting local business and political leaders, vendors, current residents, and prior visited customers. We designed flyers and a newsletter brochure and marketed with them in the general market area. Door prizes, gifts, contests, a Disc Jockey and food were all part of the strategy. But of all this, it was the precision planning and execution that made this event a success. Be willing to think outside the box and be willing to spend some money to make money. In this particular situation the prizes, food, and gifts were donated by the local businesses because they were getting plugs on the radio by the DJ. The total cost was minimized and the payback on this investment was very rewarding. This particular community gained 19% in occupancy in just 76 days as a result of the combined marketing strategies, and the open house.

You can solve the soft market problem with this Playbook. The strategies and concepts outlined in this book will give you the information, ideas, and tools you need for success. It will be up to you to do the sweat and implement them.

The Seasonality Solution

Excuse number two is seasonality. Many businesses are subjected to seasonality in the market place. Seasonality is defined as a time of year when "business" is expected to decline due to market conditions, lack of demand and customers. This is typical in markets with extreme weather conditions, and/or economic imbalances. Many traditional marketers and marketers in the ivory tower suffering from the edifice complex spend their time writing reports about why they are not meeting the financial goals and will make a list of excuses to justify their position. They often blame seasonality. This is where you will turn into a radical marketer and spend your time getting out there to fix it rather than succumb to a list of excuses.

The solution is, do marketing. Just because the market area is subjected to seasonality, make it the other guy's problem, meaning the competition's problem.

Seasonality is not a legitimate excuse to avoid marketing because "if you market, they will come" regardless of season. If you continue marketing and even step up your marketing during seasonality, you will get results. In times of seasonality the typical marketing professional and their budget conscious supervisors scale back expenses. They argue that if the income is not there, they cannot afford the expense. The expense is marketing and since marketing is on the budget as an expense, it is often the first to get cut resulting in lost profits.

A Field Experience…An example of a seasonality solution is when we repositioned a community in a predominantly college area by knowing when to say no. This particular market over several years allowed the customer to define the lease terms and as a result every community in this market carved themselves a big chunk of the vacancy pie at predictable times of the year. Because of the fear of dictating a lease term that the "student" might reject, this community and its competition ate vacancy pie year after year, until our community was finally ready and willing to say no. We said no by not allowing leases to expire at the predictable move out times and only offered certain length lease terms. If the customer could not be flexible with the new lease terms they were told no and sent away. Certainly as a marketer it is not wise to send customers away but any situation of repositioning from seasonality fate, you may have to. By mapping out when we would allow a certain amount and percentage of leases to expire we were able to define and accomplish occupancy pie. Patience is a virtue in this recovery strategy. You may have to wait until some of the competition absorbs some units. But simultaneously you must continue with an intense marketing strategy to get your piece of the market share. You will remain stable at the next seasonality turn whereas your competition will be scrambling again for occupancy.

Get Your Market Share

Many throw in the towel during these periods of seasonality and a soft market instead of challenging themselves and the market. Many marketing professionals fail to recognize this great opportunity. The opportunity is to win the most market share. In any market, regardless of seasonality or a soft market, there is market share. Market share in this case is defined as the amount of customers that are in need of your product and/or service in the general market area. It is rare for a market to have zero demand. For real estate, somebody is always moving their home or office no matter where you are. It is your job to find out whom and convince them to buy from you. You will accomplish this by doing marketing that reaches them. The end result is, seasonality and a soft market will become the other guys problem; meaning your competition's problem.

Success Breeds Competition

In a highly competitive seasonality or soft market, success will breed competition. New and stronger competition can come from any direction and they should not be underestimated.

Once you implement this Playbook and execute it with precision, competition will increase. This is especially true in a soft market where most competitors are reduced to offering a sale or concession as their primary, and usually the only marketing tactic because it is all they know how to do. Most will react to your strategies by increasing their sale or concession. Do not let this take you off course, stick to the Playbook.

There are 2 ways to approach the competition: the "dog-eat-dog" way or the "neighborly" way and there is no hard-and-fast proof that either strategy is better. For real estate, you may choose to split your competition; half will receive your dog-eat-dog strategy and the other half will receive your neighborly strategy. For instance the dog-eat-dog competitors can be direct mailed and more heavily solicited whereas the neighborly competition will receive your product brochures and visa versa and you can share customers with them. It is rare to have a neighborly strategy with all your competition because there is always dogs out there and these dogs, no matter how neighborly you are, will relish at any opportunity to prey on your customers.

An example of a real estate dog-eat-dog tactic is to choose one or two of your top competition and direct mail them with the daily or Sunday paper (one-time) delivered to their door. You can design a flyer and stuff it inside the paper. The message on the flyer is critical to its effectiveness. It should clearly state whom it is from and why it was sent. If it is confusing as to whom the flyer is from, you could have an unintended consequence. One time a community tried this tactic and the flyer did not boldly mention who the newspaper was compliments of, not being designed for the mind and as a result many residents actually thought their community delivered it to them. An outpouring of appreciation to their current Community Manager's office was the result. If you plan to take on such guerrilla tactics, be sure to inform the recipient that it is from you, the place down the street!

According to C. Britt Beemer's research "in 1988, 36-43% of consumers looked at newspaper inserts, by 1996 that number has grown to 74-78%."[3] Even by today that number has been significantly increased. Newspaper inserts usually reaching pre-determined zip codes, whether inserted by you and delivered to the competition in a dog-eat-dog guerrilla tactic or provided as a service by the newspaper, should not be underestimated. When used effectively you can achieve significant results and its cost is minimal.

An example of a neighborly tactic is to send lunch to the competition for sending you customers that result in a lease and/or sale. Offer such things as gift certificates, movie tickets, or lottery tickets; all equally effective. In some states such rewards are unlawful.

When a competitor appears to be in trouble don't celebrate; beware. At first it may appear that there is one fewer competition but rather it is a warning sign. A worthy opponent's troubles can take a turn for the worse. A troubled competitor in desperation will take risks and you may be added to their dog-eat-dog list. Even during periods when your business is thriving and the competition is doing poorly you are still vulnerable. I call this occupancy arrogance. Occupancy arrogance occurs when a business scales back all marketing efforts and cuts the marketing budget the minute they hit their sales goal. This penny-wise pound-foolish budget cutting strategy costs more than its price. The price is lost business and the cost is reduced profits. By the time a business notices it is in "marketing" trouble, valuable time has been lost. Companies should come to understand the concept of sustained marketing. Sustained marketing is when you continue marketing and advertising your product and/or services regardless of your current sales and positive financial situation so you are continually providing your business with future new customer opportunities. It is important to continue to market your business to new future customers so you can draw from them in the event you have a downturn in business.

In addition, when a competitor is in trouble somebody may be ready to post bail, such as a new owner and/or company with new capital, guaranteed to have a fresh perspective on the marketplace and declare war. Beware of them especially.

No Excuses
The real estate owners that hire professionals to put heads on beds and derrieres at desks will not and should not tolerate the seasonality or soft market excuse. For those of you that are the marketing professional and are using the seasonality or soft market excuse, first, nobody wants to hear what you can not do; they want to hear about what you can do.

Second, and equally important, you are not implementing rule #9; "If you market, they will come." A solution-oriented marketing professional can solve a seasonality or soft market issue. We can solve it because we are willing to sweat and the competition is not. One of the problems with the marketing industry today is that many are stuck in the traditional marketing approach and are surrendering to seasonality and soft markets. You will need to become a radical marketing thinker to overcome seasonality or a soft market.

Brokers

If you are being proactive towards the seasonality and/or soft market solution and are accomplishing it by hustling to market in the business community, you are a millennium marketer. But if you are accomplishing this through only utilizing brokers, i.e. realtors, and apartment locators, you are utilizing one of the highest cost per result marketing solicitation strategies. These referral sources will continue in the new millennium but you should begin to implement a variety of the play-book tactics so you are not so heavily relying on these referral sources to bring you customers.

Although futurists say that new technology advancements will create a reduction in the use of brokers, there will still be an end user market share. Regardless of the ability to easily access and seek the information themselves by way of the Internet, many customers will not elect to perform this self-service. It is a fact that the Internet is impacting brokers but it will not eliminate the use of them.

The brokers present the real estate industry with a significantly higher cost per result than other marketing sources do and there is much to gain by reducing the use of them. However, we still need them by virtue of our customers' use of them. Brokers will likely be forced to reevaluate and readjust their fee structures. A message to the brokers is rather than accepting a cut off when occupancy is strong in a real estate market, it is wiser to negotiate for a minimum referral base. Although the brokers need the marketers business just as bad as the marketers need the brokers, if the marketer cuts these vendors out of the strategy at high time, the brokers may be more inclined to conveniently forget your business when you need them at low time. It is wise to work out a comfortable strategy agreement that reflects a win/win strategy for both parties involved.

Besides brokers, whom do we tap for more business? The answer is the business community. Not just the obvious employer business community but the general business community too.

Build a Bi-lateral Business Referral Network

Marketers do not just work for the company or themselves, they work for and represent the business community. Many businesses, especially small businesses, do not have marketing personnel departments or any idea how to reach their intended audience. By aligning yourself with the businesses in your general business community you can build a successful bi-lateral business referral network.

As you begin to implement this strategy be forewarned that many businesses will not understand your motives at first and will likely say "not interested." For one, they think you are tying to sell them something and second, it will strike them as odd that you are asking to do their marketing for them. Many will ask what you charge for the service because they are unfamiliar with the bi-lateral, networking concept so you may need to coach them on it. At this juncture, many marketers would give up and move on. As a millennium marketer you will need to exercise resilience.

Creating a bi-lateral marketing strategy by partnering with businesses has its rewards. You will benefit from their referrals and in return they will benefit from your referrals. You will be offering the businesses a marketing consultant service for no charge. You will accomplish this by learning more about their business and their desired customer and convincing them that they need you. You may say, "Yeah, with what time?" How about 15 minutes. In 15 minutes you can determine for example: the video store, grocery store, pizza place, coffee shop, clothing store, hardware store, beauty salon, vet clinic, medical center etc. is just down the street from your place of business. Would these local businesses be interested in knowing how many customers I have and how many new customers I have each month? By sharing that information we are not in breach of privacy law of our customers and we are not giving out names, ranks and serial numbers, just quantities.

Now you are ready to compile this information in a flyer type message. The marketing offer can be your brochures, newsletter, and promotional campaign, whatever you feel the business will need to refer your company. You will also want to take your testimonials along. You will want to share with your new marketing partner the results of others that have joined your bi-lateral business referral network. Many will not be able to resist this bandwagon approach.

A Field Experience…While conducting marketing for a community that was considered to be in a soft market, I entered a business in the local business community to meet with the General Manager. I was armed with a comprehensive collateral package of brochures, newsletter, flyers, coupons, testimonials, a gift, and move-ins stats, because according to the guerrilla guru, Jay Conrad Levinson "facts presented to the eye and ear are 68 percent more effective than facts presented to the ear alone."[4] This business (a major kitchen and bath accessory store; new to the market) and only 4 miles from the community, was only 3 days away from their grand opening and I wasn't going to take no for an answer. I decided to wait for the General Manager to come out of his meeting. And, it was well worth the wait. It turns out that the GM was in a marketing meeting with his Divisional Manager, and they were discussing the grand opening's sales and marketing strategies. I was in the right place at the right time but this is not such a coincidence as I have experienced many situations similar to this one. Marketing is a numbers game and if you knock on enough doors you will create these situations. The GM granted me 3 minutes of his time (he literally barked; "You got 3 minutes!)" I gave him a stat sheet of the resident employer profile, number of residents, and their average income range so he could make an informed decision as to if our customers met his targeted customer criteria. I knew it did before I went there but the win comes from letting them see it, believe it, and then make the decision as if they thought of it. I also handed him testimonials from satisfied residents and other local businesses that had joined our network strategy and resulted in an increase in business and sales. He became enthusiastic, gave me coupons, flyers, and 100 exclusive grand opening pre-view invitations with a $15 coupon for which we sent out along with a renewal letter and reminder to the first 100 expiring leases at the community. Not only did we have a retention rate of 74% of those 100 residents; 27 of those residents attended the preview event and within 3 months we had 5 of the stores employees living at this community and many future referrals as a result.

The tools you need for overcoming seasonality and a soft market, besides a radical marketing attitude and a willingness to get out there and sweat, is a bi-lateral business referral network, customer data, testimonials, and your collateral/promotional items to market with, and the remainder of this Playbook.

Chapter 10
Rule #10—Train the Troops

"Build with your team a feeling of oneness, of dependence on one another, and of strength derived from unity, in the pursuit of your objective."

—*Vince Lombardi*

From one employee to an army of employees, without training, a swarm of customers will do you no good if the team is not trained to handle them. Since this book is not about the Sales discipline what is meant by "Training the Troops" is to introduce the marketing strategy into their world with a new TEAM training approach and ensuring they understand the "why" of tracking customer data for the database.

What's in it for them?
Everybody needs to know the marketing strategy and you are closer to the results if you deliver it to them in terms in which they understand and by defining what's in it for them for doing it.

Many people have considerable abilities that are often underdeveloped. We need to find and develop whatever talent they have. People love training. It builds their confidence. Train them to be millennium marketers.

People will need to be motivated. Since motivation is different for everyone you will need to find out what their motivated by and then you can clearly prescribe what their end game experience and reward will be.

Get a new TEAM

An effective manner in which to introduce the marketing plan to the team is to market the plan to them with a new team. You may be familiar with the TEAM concept—Together Each Achieves More. It grew in popularity in the past decade and although it is another trite rite people are bored with it. To rejuvenate the TEAM, get a new TEAM. Not by replacing the team but by getting a new TEAM concept because—Together Each Achieves More is out and—Technology Equipment Activates Membership is in.

The new TEAM:

>   Technology
>   Equipment
>   Activates
>   Membership

Technology—To prosper in the new millennium you should train on technology. Every employee should have access to the Internet. In real estate, it is crucial to have access at the community level. Since your marketing plan will involve the Internet, the team should fully understand it. If you are a real time organization, you should train them on the real time system. They also should be trained on how the software program is used and all the intricacies of how the marketing is tracked by the computer. You should train the team on the 5 T's to Tracking from Chapter Six and introduce them to all the Internet advertising you and the competition are using.

Equipment—Also knows as toys. The millennium employee wants toys. Internet access, real time, software upgrades, and all the latest and greatest available tools on the market to make their job not just easier but more fun, effective and worthwhile. You will need to make an equipment list. With this list you will be prepared to explain to the team how much easier it will be to accomplish the marketing tasks. For example: they will likely be making flyers, so get them the latest desk top publishing software and install it on their computer. Set them up with a postage machine if your plan involves heavy direct mailing, follow-up, business to business mailings, and get them set up on an express mailing account such as Airborne or Federal Express. This is the millennium sell of "time" for your customers as we explored in Chapter Two. Give them the Cost Per Result (CPR) and the Payback Axiom (PA) forms or by technology. Make their job easier. If you make their job easier, the marketing is more likely to get accomplished.

Activate—When you activate, your taking action. Employees are usually bored with status quo anyway so if you give them a plan to activate you will likely receive a gusto reaction. You will get this reaction if you convince them that by activating they will get an experience and a reward. Too many marketing plans lose their gusto at this stage. Most people need to have their activation button pushed. After you thoroughly review the marketing plan, activate their action button by giving them the 5th P—Physical action list along with their toys. Assign names and delegate responsibility. Accomplish this by trying to match the skill level of each person with the appropriate marketing assignment.

Membership—The marketing team has exclusive membership to the results. Those responsible from planning to implementing from measuring to debriefing of success, are the only ones all-inclusive to the membership and the end game results. This is where you will market with the motivation factor. What is in it for them? You will need to design an incentive plan. Incentives come in many shapes and sizes. Ask them what the end game reward should be.

For example: Ask each team member to write down what they believe is rewarding and reasonable for attaining their goal. By doing this it is likely you will get a different response from each person because people have different motivation needs. Review each response with the employee and make any necessary revisions that are agreeable to both you and the employee. It will also be important to ensure that the value of the reward is the same for all team members. Once you accomplish this you will have a realistic incentive plan. The goals are sure to be met and exceeded because the team created it. The end game goal becomes more worthwhile to each team member since the incentive is "tailor made" for them.

If you have yet to design "tailor made" incentive plans for your team members, give it a try, and see how often the goals are reached and exceeded as a result.

Training on the Database

In Chapter Six, we identified the 5 Training Techniques of Tracking; #2 is the most compelling of them and will take additional training for the new TEAM concept to be effective. #2 describes "Train the team and develop a strategy on how to complete the customer card with the customer and the process of getting all the customer data in a conversational manner and most importantly "why" we need the information; to ensure successful marketing strategies as a result of measured customer data." Our focus will be the "why." When teams are not trained on the "why," it is common for them to ignore the concept and unknowingly corrupt the "tracking" of the data.

For many industries, the customer tracking comes in the form of a customer card also known as a visitor card and/or guest card. We use the information from this card to create a database of customer contact information. Our extensive marketing effort results in generating these customers to our company in order to obtain the customer's "personal information." If it is not clearly defined to the team that the use of these cards is not just for a "sales" purpose but rather a "marketing" purpose, it is likely they will not recognize the full potential. We must train the team on the measurement discipline of "why;" it's one of the most critical components of any marketing strategy. When team members are not trained on the "why" of the tracking for the database, you will be losing valuable business.

A Field Experience…A major department store has set up a database of customer information and are asking the customers zip code to identify where the best market is to mail their advertisements to and track marketing. I gathered this from standing in line (3 customers ahead of me) while the sales clerk was asking the first customer for their zip code. When the customer asked "why" the clerk responded by saying, "I don't know, they came in last week and changed all our computers, nobody told me why we're just supposed to ask you for your zip code." Before the customer could answer the clerk with her zip code the clerk was replying "oh never mind, I'll just use a made up one," and he did. The next customer was not asked for their zip code, I assume the clerk used the same made up one. The third customer in line, having witnessed this, offered to give her zip code to the clerk and the clerk replied "no that's okay I'll keep using this one." I was the fourth customer and as a professional marketer and an advocate of customer tracking, I was disappointed at this company's failure to train this employee. And not to mention the fact that their lack of training would directly effect me; by not receiving sale ads from a store that I frequent. I decided to ask the clerk if it had to do with the companies need to know who their customers are so they can get sale ads to them and track their marketing. And he replied "I dunno," and I replied "I bet it is so and I would appreciate receiving your sale ads so please use my zip code, Thank You."

Since this company has not trained their front line people about the database tracking methods, this company is losing valuable business and is likely wasting significant marketing dollars as a result.

A Field Experience…Recently, I went to a major drug store to process some film in one hour. I frequent this store and do get asked my phone number before the sale is rang up. But this time, as the clerk entered my phone number he replied " Mrs. Blanton will you be needing double prints again." I was impressed, as I have always asked for double prints. I was curious if it had to do with the database so I asked. He replied "We have a database of all your film purchases and you have never not asked for double prints." This store has taken the time to train its front line employees on the database methods and more importantly how to use it effectively.

The underlying principles in these 2 field experiences are the same regardless of its diverse application in other industry use of database tracking methods. How much valuable business and unnecessary marketing dollars are being spent at your business as a result of inaccurate data as a result of failure to train the team on "why?"

The new millennium perk

Companies that train in technology are the leaders since technology is one of the new TEAM training approaches. A recommendation to the industry is to add Internet access at home for the employees as the new millennium perk.

By giving the employees Internet access at home as a new employment "perk," they will be less inclined to use work time to surf. This is a growing concern of many companies. Those that are getting connected for means of electronic mail and commerce communication are often experiencing a reduction in employee productivity.

A Field Experience…I was shopping a competitor and as I entered the office a group of employees were in front of the computer "surfing." After waiting for 10 minutes, one said, "oh we're sorry, we are just so excited we have the Internet now that we wanted to find out all about it." I went along with this by saying something like "Oh, that's Okay, it's fascinating isn't it?" One said, "Yes it is, and we have done nothing else for the past 3 days but surf, we are trying to learn how to find and buy stuff on it, none of us have it at home." While two of them stayed at the computer, one ended up showing me an apartment. The entire tour conversation was about the Internet. The Leasing Consultant was still so engrossed that she did not try to sell the apartment product.

Companies can avoid this unproductive scenario by getting their employee's the millennium perk; Internet access at home. No matter how hard you try to stop this behavior, as long as there is the Internet hubbub you will lose employee productivity. A written policy, corrective counseling and discipline are a band-aid to the problem, not a solution. You should approach this new phenomenon head on with a good faith measure. It will disarm them and send a message "You can surf, but not on my time."

Chapter 11
Rule #11—Form Marketing Partnerships

*"If I have seen further, it is by standing
on the shoulders of giants."*
—Sir Isaac Newton

One of the most valuable assets to any industry is the many talented and dedicated professionals that provide the tools and services to fuel our success. These unsung heroes are the vendors. In this Chapter, we will discuss what it takes to develop a marketing partnership with these vendors and I will define their responsibility to you and list the items you should request in your MRFP (Marketing Request for Proposal.)

The Win/Win Approach

Businesses need to acknowledge how much of an implicit role the marketing vendors play and how much more effective we are because of them. Marketing success is a shared success and must be approached with a win/win attitude. "With a win/win solution, all parties feel good about the decision and feel committed to the action plan."[1] The vendors depend upon us for our business but we are equally dependent on them. What would marketing professionals do without their marketing partners?

Marketing Partners

If you want to be successful in the new millennium you should form marketing partnerships. The marketing vendors will not only provide you with the specific services you hired them for. If you communicate the desire to take a more active role in the success of their business, you will be rewarded with more than just a service but rather a partnership that goes beyond their normal scope of service. Taking an active role can include such things as writing testimonials when you and your marketing partner have a successful campaign and offering to be a referral source with their new clients. Although many vendors will form a marketing partnership with you regardless of your testimonials and business referrals you should still be an active participant in the success of their business as well as yours.

By forming a marketing partnership, your partner will keep you up to date on trends, ideas, and new information that you may have missed. Trends, such as in occupancy, or new employers moving into the market place, and new construction announcements, are all examples of information you will be fed as a result of a marketing partnership.

Marketing vendors must sell time

Marketing vendors that want a marketers business must know as much about their advertisers, and as much if not more than the advertiser knows about its customers. Since marketer's goals in the new millennium have changed from frequency to relevance with the new results maxim, the marketing vendors must find ways to "sell time" to the marketer.

When a marketing vendor solicits you with their product or service offering they should be equipped with a clear, concise, and comprehensive database and/or demographic analysis of a targeted audience as well as other materials you need to make a decision. If not, you simply will not have the time to see them. Which results in missed marketing opportunities for you and missed sales opportunities for your vendor.

In order to be productive with marketing vendors and efficient with my time I developed what I call a MRFP (Marketing Request For Proposal.) The MRFP is a list of items that I request from the vendor to either provide me with prior to our meeting and/or to bring to the meeting. The items included on the MRFP list are:

1. Company history, time in business, and a current reference list.
2. Testimonials.
3. Database information with clear and concise information on the targeted audience, demographic analysis, distribution, and tracking mechanisms, etc.
4. Samples of work.
5. Association membership.
6. Comparative analysis of their top 3 competitors. Why is their product and/or service better?
7. List of deadline and/or production schedule preferably on a calendar.
8. Identify the best form of communication, e-mail, pager, voice mail, in person, etc.
9. A contract that allows for a 30 day written cancellation by either party and certificate of insurance (if applicable) naming the marketers company as "additional insured."
10. Return on Investment data from other clients if available.

You should keep a folder and/or a binder of all your marketing vendors, their products and services, contracts, and insurance. Keep this information organized and up to date. A tickler file is best.

By utilizing your time with marketing vendors more effectively and efficiently you are enabling yourself more time for participating in the actual performance of your marketing programs. Many marketers are of the school of thought that all vendors are just sales people that bother us for our time and business. The truth is these vendors often have great marketing products and/or services with a fresh perspective that you have yet to experiment with. But if you grant all of them a meeting without preparation, you will be buried. Utilize the MRFP list to better maximize yours and the vendor's time.

You should expect to receive data-driven provable results from marketing vendors soliciting for your business. Marketing vendors that want to earn a millennium marketer's business must be willing to provide, at the minimum, the information listed in the MRFP.

When marketing vendors identify the best prospects for an advertiser they have added value and will be rewarded with more business. Marketing vendors have much to gain by the development and use of a database in which to provide such information as demographic and psycho-graphic data, zip codes, age, income and most importantly any trend information on customer buying habits.

It is up to the advertiser (marketer) to set the level of expectation. The vendor can not be expected to meet the level of expectation if it is not set up front. Many vendor/marketer relationships fail because the marketer fails to communicate their wants and needs, and in almost every case, it is the vendor who suffers. Lack of communication on behalf of the marketer is unproductive. The marketing relationship is dependent on the marketing professional's ability to communicate their expectations. It is okay to be a demanding marketer when you have formed a marketing partnership because they will know where you stand on what is expected.

The Vendor Questionnaire

At your company, if you are interested in learning about the level of communication your vendors receive from your marketers or other employees, simply conduct a survey. And while you are at it, ask them about how they are treated by all the members of the staff. You will get on the pulse of how your staff treats customers by taking the pulse of the vendors.

Marketing Vendor Leadership

A Field Experience...I was contacted by an outside research and consulting firm to be interviewed on the services that a major rental guide provides. This company was in search of their customer's feedback on the service they provide as well as their competitor's service. The research interview included an opportunity for me to be open and candid about what I expect from this vendor and to offer suggestions on how the company can better serve me as a marketer. I recognized the interview would be beneficial to both parties and an opportunity to share information that not only could better my company's marketing effectiveness, but my marketing partner's business as well. You should also be willing to spend the time, no matter how time-starved you are, to form and nourish such marketing partnerships.

Chapter 12
Rule #12—The Law of Unintended
Consequences

"They may forget what you said,
but they will never forget how you made
them feel."

—Carl W. Buechner

As you begin to implement Rules #1-11, you will be generating specific slogans, campaigns, names, and concepts that will co-exist with your overall strategy. During the quest for results it is not uncommon to receive unintended results or consequences when you do not employ the discipline of pre-search. The Law of Unintended Consequences, Rule #12, deals in the outcome of a slogan, campaign tactic, or idea that was not ultimately received as it was intended. You cannot completely predict how your idea will be received, but by performing pre-search, you can avoid many downside unintended consequences.

The Pinto
When the Pinto was introduced in Brazil the marketer did not know that the term Pinto was Brazilian slang for "small male genitalia." Likely this is not the image they had in mind. It failed miserably. When you are naming a product, service, slogan, floor plans/models, or a slogan for a new flyer or campaign, the actual words meanings, and potential slang, must be researched.

I'd like to teach the world to sing

The next example of the Law of Unintended Consequences is about an advertising campaign by Coca-Cola. Do you remember this commercial—I'd like to teach the world to sing in perfect harmony, I'd like to buy the world a Coke and keep it company. Sergio Zyman, a brilliant marketer and the author of The End of Marketing as We Know It, only states the first few words of the commercial in his book, but I was able to finish the harmony because I remembered it from childhood. It was enduring. It embraced diversity. Children and adults from all ages and races were joined together in unity and everyone loved it. It was disappointing to learn that it was one of Coca-Colas worst advertising campaigns. In fact, Coke lost market share the entire time the commercial ran. Despite this feel good campaign at a time of mass movement to diversification and unity, it did not sell more Coke. From a moral perspective this commercial, although its intention was to sell more Coke, sold the world on its need to become one and promoted unity. The diversity message overshadowed the product. Although Coke's sales were down after such a campaign if anyone's sales went up it was Disney's and any other organization that was positioned at the time to benefit from an outpouring of unity do-gooders. The Coke commercial was favored by many but it did not do its marketing job; to sell more Coke and get results.

Drama Sells

Coke and Pepsi continually re-position themselves. Pepsi won the market position as the best value after the sugar crisis in 1975. Both soft drinks raised their prices but when the crisis ended Pepsi rolled back their prices and Coke did not. Then Bill Cosby arrives on the scene with "The Real Thing" campaign and shortly after that "Coke is It" emerged. In turn, Pepsi positioned itself as the "new generation," implying that Coke was consumed by the old folks. The world was watching when Michael Jackson's hair caught on fire as he introduced Pepsi's new generation commercial. It was dramatic and drama sells.

Thanks Kid

Keeping with the cola theme, in the Mean Joe Greene Coke commercial, "Mean Joe Greene, injured and mad"[1] after a game is offered a Coke from a boy. Mean Joe Greene says "Thanks Kid" and tosses the kid his jersey. Everybody loved it. The critic's raved. But the ad was not selling more Coke so it was pulled. This feel good campaign mainly for all fathers and sons alike lived on. But the benefactor of this unintended result was probably the NFL because fathers and sons flocked to the stadiums to live out their own kind of experience.

The Mating Call

The New England railroad industry had no prediction of their unintended consequence when they changed the whistle on the railroad trains in an effort to improve safety at crossings. The new whistle proved irresistible to the areas moose population and they took it as a mating call and unfortunately many were killed on the tracks. Irresistible marketing to the five senses, one being hearing does not only appeal and apply to humans.

The Chevy Nova Awards

There is actually an award for The Law of Unintended Consequence in advertising and marketing. It is called the Chevy Nova Award named in honor of General Motor's fiasco in trying to market this car in Central and South America. "Nova" in Spanish means, "it doesn't go." Needless to say, it didn't go well. Although there have been many nominations for this award, I have only listed a few:

The Dairy Associations huge success campaign "Got Milk?" prompted them to expand advertising to Mexico. It was soon brought to their attention that the Spanish translation read, "Are you lactating?"

Coors Beer put its slogan, "Turn It Loose," into Spanish, where it translated as, "Suffer from Diarrhea."

Frank Perdue's chicken, "It takes a strong man to make a tender chicken" was translated into Spanish as, "It takes an aroused man to make a chicken affectionate."

When Parker Pen marketed a ballpoint pen in Mexico, its ads were supposed to have read, "It won't leak in your pocket and embarrass you." The company thought that the word "embarazar" (to impregnate) meant to embarrass, so the ad read, "It won't leak in your pocket and make you pregnant."

When American Airlines wanted to advertise its new first class leather seats in the Mexican market, its "Fly in Leather" campaign became, "Fly Naked" (vuela en cuero) in Spanish.

Other marketing translation goof-ups:

Scandinavian vacuum manufacturer Electrolux used the following in an American campaign, "Nothing sucks like an Electrolux."

Clairol introduced the "Mist Stick" a curling iron, into German only to find out that "mist" is slang for manure. Not too many people had use for the "manure stick."

Colgate introduced a toothpaste in France called "Cue," the name of a notorious porno magazine.

Pepsi's "Come alive with the Pepsi Generation" translated into Chinese as, "Pepsi brings your ancestors back from the grave."

Conclusion

Throughout this book a common theme has prevailed; lead or migrate. The Marketing discipline, the solicitation of new customers, is all-inclusive. The absence of one chapter's implementation is counterproductive to the final results. In marketing, there is no easy way, you must do the sweat. I would be remiss if I did not warn you of the potential dangers of applying these rules while being surrounded by naysayers and habitants of the ivory tower suffering from the edifice complex. My favorite quote and best advice for this situation is to remember this quote:

> "Great Spirits have always encountered violent opposition from mediocre minds"
> by Albert Einstein.

For the Leaders, these 12 rules will most likely fill the void in your relentless pursuit of the "quick fix" subsequently affording you the time to redirect your attention to implementation of these 12 rules while questioning and challenging them along the way. By questioning and challenging them you are leading rather than migrating. They also imply a change and in many cases, radical changes. Even if you are operationally excellent you will need to continually raise the bar. You will need these cover-to-cover concepts to stay in the game of results.

For the Migrators, these 12 rules, by the virtue of their commitment to print, will affirm your thinking that by just having the rules, it evens the playing field. These 12 rules will fill the void of your quest for taking the easy way out because there is no easy way out in marketing. You must do the sweat.

Now that you have read the 12 rules, go out and discover a few of your own. Perform some experiments and be willing to take risks. Those that continue to rush into meetings to come up the marketing flavor of the week should think instead about spending their time implementing these 12 rules.

It is inevitable that rules will get broken. Rules are not only to be followed but also to be challenged and questioned. As Vince Lombardi said, "Don't just stand there, hit something."

About the Author

Victoria L. Blanton was born and raised in Seattle, Washington. She has been a resident of Central Florida for the past 12 years. Her accreditations are CAM, ARM, and NALP. She is presently in the real estate industry and specializes in Marketing.

Notes

Chapter 1—Source Notes

[1]Predatory Marketing; C. Britt Beemer; page 14—"a marketing strategy that was 100% effective in the 1980's will have lost 84-96% of its effectiveness today."

[2]The End of Marketing as We Know It by Sergio Zyman; direct quote "debrief your success; equally important, and perhaps more valuable than analyzing and correcting things that turn out to be wrong is analyzing and building on the things that go right."

[3]Guerrilla Marketing Weapons by Jay Conrad Levinson; direct quote page 43 "in a research study designed to show prime influences, confidence came in first, quality came in second, service came in third, and selection came in fourth, price came in ninth."

[4]Predatory Marketing; C. Britt Beemer; "the percentage of customers who try to get a lower price by mentioning other stores, whether or not they have actually shopped is 59%."

Chapter 2—Source Notes

[1]The Discipline of Market Leaders; Choose your Customers, Narrow Your Focus, Dominate Your Market by Michael Treacy and Fred Wiersema 1995; direct quote—Page 6 "Today's customers demand operations that are airborne, online, and in real time."

[2]Multi-Housing News; July 99 issue pages 20 and 21.

[3]Real Time; Preparing for the Age of the Never Satisfied Customer by Regis McKenna direct quote—page 6 "Real time is characterized by the shortest possible lapse between idea and reaction between initiation and result."

[4]Real Time; Preparing for the Age of the Never Satisfied Customer by Regis McKenna; "companies best equipped for the twenty-first century will consider investment in real time systems as essential to maintaining their competitive edge."

[5]Real Time; Preparing for the Age of the Never Satisfied Customer by Regis McKenna—page 3 "habits, attitudes, opinions, preferences, expectations, demands, perceptions, and needs all adapt unwittingly to an environment in which immediacy rules."

Chapter 3—Source Notes

[1]Positioning; The Battle for Your Mind by Al Ries and Jack Trout "We must do this because today, customers are no longer responding to the positioning tactics of the past."

[2]The New Marketing Era by Paul Postma; direct quote—page 107 "There is a certain order, independent of our preferences, in the way we perceive various stimuli presented to us."

[3]7 Kinds of Smart; Identifying Your Many Intelligences; Thomas Armstrong page 9-12. Howard Gardner developed the revolutionary idea that there are at least seven intelligence's worthy of mode and thought. They are Linguistic Intelligence, Logical-mathematical Intelligence, Spatial Intelligence, Musical Intelligence, Bodily-kinesthetic Intelligence, Interpersonal Intelligence, Intrapersonal Intelligence.

[4]The Experience Economy; Work is Theater and Every Business a Stage—by B. Joseph Pine II and James H. Gilmore—page 2 "When a

person buys a service, he purchases a set of intangible activities carried out on his behalf. But when he buys an experience, he pays to spend time enjoying a series of memorable events that a company stages."

[5]The Experience Economy; Work is Theater and Every Business a Stage—by B. Joseph Pine II and James H. Gilmore—pages 39-40 "Those businesses that regulate themselves to the diminishing world of goods and services will be rendered irrelevant."

[6]The Experience Economy; Work is Theater and Every Business a Stage—by B. Joseph Pine II and James H. Gilmore—pages 39-40, 4 aspects of an experience: the aesthetics aspect, the escapist aspect, the educational aspect, the entertainment aspects.

Chapter 4—Source Notes

[1]Inside the Magic Kingdom; Seven Key's to Disney's Success by Tom Connellan; direct quote "Each part that is supposed to be colored gold has been painted with 23-karat gold leaf paint."

[2]Radical Marketing by Sam Hill and Glenn Rifkin; direct quote "Branson gave the money to his employees and sent out this note: Thank You all for your help in our defense. After all, a Virgin's honor is her most prized possession."

[3]Radical Marketing; Sam Hill and Glenn Rifkin; direct quote—page 34 "the band developed unparalleled expertise in the marketing, promotion, and execution of musical events."

[4]Radical Marketing; Sam Hill and Glenn Rifkin; direct quote "Like other great radical marketers, the Dead understood the value of employees who shared the enthusiasm for the product and would in effect represent the company to the customers."

Chapter 5—Source Notes

[1]The End of Marketing as We Know it by Sergio Zyman; direct quote—page 178. "By establishing marketing as a sound business

investment marketers can get the kind of resources they need to do their jobs more effectively."

[2]The Dictionary of Theories by Jennifer Botchmley; The Law of Hype "People and institutions whose surface value (hype) is less than their substance will be driven out by those of whom the reverse is true."

[3]Guerrilla Marketing Excellence by Jay Conrad Levinson "avoid the use of humor unless it is pertinent to your offering and does not detract from your offer."

[4]Guerrilla Marketing Newsletter by Jan Conrad Levinson Volume 12 number 5 Sept-Oct. 1998; direct quote "Who are you? What is your product or service? When are you open? Where are you located? The reality is that the only real question in the customer's mind is, Why should I care?"

[5]The End of Marketing as We Know it by Sergio Zyman; direct quote - page 203 "Marketing Professionals are hired for their expertise therefore others with no marketing skills and abilities should not be commenting on or controlling the marketing activities and strategies."

[6]The End of Marketing as We Know it by Sergio Zyman; direct quote - page 203 "their opinions are valid but only in their field of expertise."

Chapter 6—Source Notes
[1]Radical Marketing by Sam Hill and Glenn Rifkin "A visceral connection to the customer, a long term commitment to the cause, and a willingness to work with and make the best of what's at hand."

[2]Radical Marketing by Sam Hill and Glenn Rifkin "visceral connection to the customer."

[3]Radical Marketing by Sam Hill and Glenn Rifkin "For many, the Harley roar is classic noise pollution. But for the Harley lovers, it is a mating call."

[4]Radical Marketing by Sam Hill and Glenn Rifkin—"A $20 million dollar business in 1988 grew to $100 million by 1996."

[5]Real Time Preparing for the Age of the Never Satisfied Customer by Regis McKenna; direct quote—page 117 "For marketing taking its cues from customer's wants and reactions, the real time tool with the most radical benefits has to do with measurement."

[6]The New Rules of Marketing; Frederick Newell; page 48— "Information is not knowledge until we analyze it and understand it. Knowledge is not power until we learn how to use it."

Chapter 7—Source Notes

[1]Radical Marketing by Sam Hill and Glenn Rifkin, direct quote "a long term commitment to the cause."

[2]Basic Concepts in Sociology by Max Weber; direct quote—page 30 "such proof of understanding will be either of rational, i.e., logical or mathematical, or of an emotionally empathic, artistic appreciative, character."

[3]Basic Concepts of Sociology by Max Weber; direct quote—page 53 "formulated with greater precision only where it is a matter of qualitatively equal behavior but differing merely in degrees."

[4]The New Marketing Era by Paul Postman; direct quote—page 102-103 "In consultative situations in which we are involved as marketing professionals, messy thinking can be recognized all too easily especially regarding critical strategic problems for which people ask our opinions."

Chapter 8—Source Notes

[1]Dictionary of Theories by Jennifer Bothamley; direct quote—page 307 "in theories of psychology, this principle states that given certain possibilities for action, an organism will select the one requiring the least effort."

[2]The New Rules of Marketing; Frederick Newell—page 149 "At a National Center for the 79thAnnual DMA (Direct Mailing Association) conference in New Orleans, October 1996; 16 successful new loyalty marketing programs were introduced."

[3]The End of Marketing as We Know it by Sergio Zyman; direct quote— page 90 "it helps you control the dialogue in the market by defining the standards for judgement; and it narrows the position of your competition to an area where it is weaker than you are."

[4]The New Rules of Marketing; Frederick Newell—page 92 "The more you use it and learn the better it performs if you do your homework."

Chapter 9—Source Notes

[1]Predatory Marketing; C. Britt Beemer—page 208 "94% of people believe a grand opening sale is legitimate."

[2]Predatory Marketing; C. Britt Beemer—page 211 "can generate 50-60% of what an original grand opening can."

[3]Predatory Marketing; C. Britt Beemer- page 49 "in 1988, 36-43% of consumers looked at newspaper inserts. By 1996 that number has grown to 74-78%."

[4]Guerrilla Weapons; Jay Conrad Levinson- page 69 "facts presented to the eye and ear are 68 percent more effective than facts presented to the ear alone."

Chapter 10—Source Notes

None

Chapter 11—Source Notes

[1]The 7 Habits of Highly Effective People by Stephen R. Covey; direct quote page 207 "With a win/ win solution, all parties feel good about the decision and feel committed to the action plan."

Chapter 12—Source Notes

[1]The End of Marketing as We Know It by Sergio Zyman; "Mean Joe Greene, injured and mad."

Glossary

Acquisition: The process of gaining possession of an asset through management and ownership.

A la Carte: A list of separate marketing items to be utilized or displayed as options available for a marketing program.

Beds: The term used to describe the number of units at a real estate asset/community and/or the number of rooms at a community. The term is common when describing student housing with for instance 4 bedrooms in one unit resulting in 4 beds.

Bandit Signs: They used to be called bootleg signs; they are small signs promoting a business via directions, amenities, phone number, etc.

Bi-lateral Marketing Strategy: A networking opportunity to businesses that refer their customers and employees to your business and in return you advertise and market their products and services to your customers. The relationship is established by the marketer through outreach. You can create a bi-lateral marketing strategy by partnering with businesses. You will accomplish this by learning more about their business and their desired customer and convincing them that they need you.

Brite Rite: A term used for something that is a new and good idea and proven right.

Broker: A person or company that provides customers with the service of locating your business, products and/or services that saves the customer time from conducting their own research. In the real estate application of the term, they provide future customers with the service of assisting them in locating office space and/or a home or apartment. There is a referral fee charged usually to the company.

Butts in Seats: Is a term used by the airlines as a goal to put peoples "Butts" in seats thus generating profit for the company.

Buzzword: A word or phrase connected with a specialized field that is used especially to impress laypersons. It's usually worthy of attention and popularized in finance and politics but is universal to all industries.

Collateral Package: The brochure and informational materials that are a collective works and assembled as a whole. They usually have continuity with each other. The product usage of paper, for instance, would all match in color, style, and content.

Concession: A discount or a special offered to a customer to lure them to buying now by discounting the price.

Course Correction: A course correction is when you need to deviate from your stated plan according to the new results or any undesired outcome that presents itself while your plan is underway.

Curb Experience Appeal: Curb appeal has been widely defined as the appearance of a business from a drive by perspective and/or the curb. Landscaping, parking area, signage, and the overall look of the area are considered to be either positive or negative. The goal is to accomplish positive curb appeal, by engaging the customer, and connecting with them in a memorable way, creating an experience that they will not forget from encountering your business. In the curb experience appeal, the 4 aspects of an experience play a role; esthetics, escapist, entertainment, and educational.

Debrief Success: The process of analyzing and questioning the outcome of a mission to determine its effectiveness in order to repeat the performance.

Derrieres at Desks: A term I use to describe the goal of the commercial real estate industry; to fill up their office space by putting peoples derrieres (or Butts) at desks thus generating profit for the company.

Differentiation: The marketing approach to make your product and/or offering different from the competitions for the customer in order to make an informed decision.

Discipline: A controlled act in marketing of a particular skill performed on a regular basis.

Dog-eat-dog Marketing: The manner in which a business competes and is predatory with the area competition resulting in luring customers away. A tactic that is used against your competition that increases the customer opportunity to buy from you rather than the competition and/or steal sales away from the competition to increase your business.

Double Truck: The term used for the use of 2 pages in an advertising publication to accomplish a larger ad and more information.

Economic Offering: A science concerned with the consumption or use of goods and services often of the financial aspect.

Edifice Complex: The edifice complex is a syndrome where the sufferer demonstrates a need to receive data that agrees with what they think and an inability to get out of the tower and check. The data therefore becomes marketing's detriment. The discipline of accurately measuring marketing increases the Marketing disciplines ability to produce results. Inaccurate reporting of data drastically reduces marketing's opportunity to be improved. If it can not be measured properly it can not be improved. Many marketing inhabitants of the ivory tower suffer from this complex.

Educational Experience: The educational aspect is accomplished by marketing with the active aspect. Tell them what type of events will unfold before them. Let the solicited customer know it requires their participation. Inform them of the potential for newly acquired knowledge and skills.

Electronic Commerce (e-commerce): The process for which goods and services can be bought and sold electronically through the Internet.

Entertainment Experience: The entertainment aspect is self-explanatory. Let the solicited customer know what you can do to provide them with entertainment and engage the customer by explaining how they can have more fun and memorable times.

Escapist Experience: The escapist aspect is accomplished by engaging them into activities. They will be in an immersive state. Let the solicited customer know what the "thrill" will be. Also you will need to satisfy their interest in knowing what to do if they participate. They will want to be prepared.

Esthetic Experience: The esthetic experience is an aspect describing what type of environment they will experience when they visit, how inviting and comfortable it will be, and marketing to their hidden need to have a place to "just hang out." In esthetic experiences individuals will also become immersed in the moment.

Experience Economy: The experience economy is an offering to the customer that exceeds the standard expectations of customers and engages them with an experience that allows you to connect with them in a personal and memorable way. The experience economy is not just about goods and services but rather providing customers with an experience.

Fall-Out: The number of customers that will give notice based on your average monthly turnover ratio.

Field Experience: Used in this book as an introduction to a real life marketing experience that I have encountered.

Field of Dreams Strategy: "If you build it, they will come" is a phrase popularized from the hit movie "Field of Dreams," featuring baseball legends of the past. The word "build" was modified to mean "build real estate" in the use of the word. The word "market" was modified to mean "market your product and/or services" as a process of acting out marketing and the customers will "come" to you.

Fish where the fish are: Applying more marketing and advertising money and energy in an area that is currently bringing positive results.

Fluff Puff Factor (FP): The fluff puff factor is defined as a marketing tactic that is a low cost investment but lacks substance, which usually results in loss of credibility especially when used for the wrong target audience.

Futurist: An analytical person who relates current processes to the future and predicts future outcomes.

Grand Opening: A planned opening event that invites the public to experience and preview the offering in a hospitable manner. Usually an event to introduce a brand new business to the market. The event is usually marketed over a period of time and builds up to the final "opening" date.

Guerrilla Marketing: A process that approaches marketing with intensity, determination, and perseverance, and operating in many territories with a militant attitude to out market and lure customers away from the competition.

Heads on Beds: Is a term used in the multi-family real estate industry as a goal to remain "occupied" by having peoples "heads" on their beds thus resulting in profit for the company.

Imagineer: A term used by Disney for the process of coming up with new ideas, products, services, and offering them to the public for profit and/or an "experience."

Intensity: A manner in which one is performing strong in quality and degree, employing much effort and concentration.

Law of Unintended Consequences: When a marketing idea does not result in the manner in which it was intended resulting in an unplanned outcome.

Leader: A person or organization that is in the front position, innovative, leads, directs, and/or guides processes ahead of everyone else.

Lip Service: Happens when a person communicates a marketing source or idea that they think generates the most customers because it is what they remembered or liked, in absence of checking the proven outcome.

Location, Location, Location: Phraseology of a positioning strategy common in real estate and retail. Location is described as the physical place where something is situated. When shown three times it further exemplifies its meaning. It was the foremost marketing strategy of the 1990's. It became an idea that everyone embraced and bought into. You seldom pick up an advertising piece, newspaper, or real estate publication today without seeing Location, Location, Location in the headline.

Marketing: The discipline of soliciting new customers to a business and providing the opportunity for buying or selling your product, services, and ideas by reaching out to customers needs and preferences whether initiated by the customer or not.

Marketing Menu: The complete list of marketing items to be utilized for a program.

Market Share: The amount of customers that are in need of your product and/or services in the general market area.

Market Survey: An analysis, usually in the form of a spreadsheet of the area competition describing each in detail and the manner in which they compete with one another.

McCarthy 4 P's: The McCarthy 4 Ps are Product, Price, Place, and Promotion. McCarthy determines these four instruments as the controllable instruments of a marketing mix.

Measuring Stick: The term used to broadly describe the methodology on how performance is measured in the new millennium. Results is the measuring stick in the new millennium.

Migrator: A person or organization that is following another person or organization. They lack direction and prefer to be guided. They often contribute to maintaining the status quo.

Millennium Marketer: A person who understands and identifies with the 12 rules outlined in this book and is willing to put them into action.

Naysayer: Is someone who sees your action, enthusiasm, and energy, as a threat and will try to convince you that you are wasting time on a problem. They believe in nothing except what has been proven to them and what they have experienced.

Nosy Busybody (NB Factor): Studies have shown that people may not read your brochure, prospectus, or your ads, but they will read a 4-color 4-page newsletter about your business. It satisfies their insatiable curiosity and the hidden need to do so. People are nosey by nature and want access to newsworthy information.

Neighborly Marketing: The manner in which a business approaches the competition by way of a cordial and warm relationship resulting in shared customers and a win/win situation for both parties.

Newsletter Brochure: A 4-page, 4-color newsletter that serves as a brochure. The front cover contains information about the business, services, amenities, a map, directions etc. The back page can be used to communicate additional information about the business and provide an area to place an address for direct mailing. The center can be used for such things as floor plans, pictures, samples of products and/or services, testimonials, etc. It is one of the least expensive, color quality brochure ideas you can use to solicit new customers.

Occupancy Arrogance: Occupancy arrogance occurs when a business scales back all marketing efforts and cuts the marketing budget the moment they hit their sales/occupancy goal. This penny-wise pound-foolish budget cutting strategy costs more than its price.

One-Stop Shop: A place that offers all inclusive service and/or benefit of a need. In this application the one-stop shop is the complete Playbook with all the marketing; solicitation of new customers tools needed to successfully implement the program.

Open House: An event to reintroduce your business to the market and invite them in for viewing in a hospitable manner. Food, refreshments, and entertainment are usually part of the program.

Outreach: The discipline of going out into the market place to visit businesses, employers etc. to promote your business to generate more customers.

Playbook: The 12 rules outlined in this book, cover to cover, is the Playbook.

Promotional Campaign: A specific promotion to market your business with a theme and a deadline for participation.

Radical Marketing: A method of marketing that is not traditional. The methods are new, innovative, challenging, and require risk and intensity to achieve results.

Recovery: The process of returning the business to a stable condition usually pertaining to an increase in sales/occupancy by implementing the Marketing discipline.

Rehabilitated: A manner in which a business is restored and upgraded to a good/new condition for a new purpose. Usually to increase value.

Results: The manner in which the business is measured by. Results is the outcome of quantity or expression obtained by calculation and efforts in a particular way resulting in profit and success for a person and/or company.

Results, Results, Results: The manner in which companies and people are measured by. Results is the measuring stick strategy. When shown three times it further exemplifies its meaning.

Retention: The discipline of servicing, soliciting, and renewing your current customers.

Renewal: The process for which a current customer signs a new contract and/or buys from you again.

Sales: Sales is the discipline of transforming Marketed customers into buyers. It is persuasive talk designed to make people buy goods or accept an idea. An event by which product, services, and ideas are sold. Sales is known as the process of "selling" a product and/or service.

Savvy: A term used to describe a person who is well informed and perceived. They are shrewd and practical.

Scope of Marketing: The three-dimensional approach that provides a basic framework for implementation. The new scope of marketing is Marketing, Sales, and Retention. Marketing is defined as the discipline of soliciting new customers, Sales as the discipline of transforming those customers into buyers, and Customer Retention as the discipline of serving, soliciting, and renewing those buyers.

Seasonality: Is defined as a time of year when business is expected to decline due to market conditions.

Selective Perception: Is when you suddenly notice more of what you are currently thinking about and wondering why you had not noticed it so much before. For example, when you are interested in buying a new car and/or just purchased one, suddenly you notice all the exact same models on the road.

Shoe leather marketing: Is the term used for soliciting new customers with your advertising materials, flyers, brochures, etc. on foot by personally visiting businesses in the market place.

Snail Mail: Due to the speed of information technology, i.e., the internet, and e-mail, the process of sending correspondence or conduction of business through the U.S. Postal Service is considered snail mail; very slow. It can affect a companies profitability due to lost sales for the time it takes to conduct a business transaction by regular mail.

Soft Market: A soft market is defined as a market that may be overbuilt (too much supply and not enough demand) in decline, or economically unbalanced.

Standard Operating Procedure (SOP). The most widely used and accepted manner in which to operate a business, by way of a common standard.

Status Quo: Is when the marketing of a business is not challenged, changed, or put into action. It is also referred to as stagnant marketing.

Sustained marketing: Is when you continue marketing and advertising your product and/or services regardless of your current sales and positive financial situation so that you are providing your business with future customer opportunities in the event that you have a downturn in business.

TEAM: The acronym for Technology Equipment Activates Membership. The TEAM training philosophy is the new millennial approach that provides the team with specific direction and initiatives in each area thus increasing the opportunity for implementation. The group

is organized to work together with this approach to implement the solicitation of new customers in an efficient, fun, and effective manner.

Techno-driven: A person who applies the methods of technology in all
interactions with other things and people. A person who prefers the use
of technology to any other means or methods.

Thinking Outside the Box: A method of doing things and thinking of
things that are not considered with the norm. A willingness to take risks
and challenge ordinary thinking and ways of doing things better and
more efficiently.

Tickler File: A file in which to organize items that cause you to
remember and calls attention to deadlines, dates, and action items.

Time Economy: A science concerning with the offering, consumption
and regard for ones time resulting in a social and/or financial gain for
a customer.

Time-starved: A term used to describe how people are limited on time
due to many professional and personal obligations leaving minimal
time to obtain information and make transactions with a company.

Total Quality Management (TQM) revolution: A movement to place
more focus on company-employee relations and customer service.
Companies new it was crucial to their success to involve their People.
In a TQM organization, employees serve customers with total quality
and empowerment.

Traditional Marketing: Beliefs in marketing that have been handed down
through generations and decades; a long established method or procedure
where challenge, risk, and intensity are minimized or obsolete.

Trickery Shield: A defense mechanism that customers use when they
encounter marketing and/or sales tactics that are overused and take
advantage of the customers. People who are in sales are known to put

up their trickery shield when they encounter sales tactics from another sales person.

Trite rite: A term used for something that is common place, overused and lacking in originality but proven to be right.

Turnover: The term used to describe the process for which you turnover/lose customers on an ongoing basis. In real estate it is usually determined by a percent of the total units and prior performance.

Universal Formula: The proven, scientific, mathematical equation that predicts the lease-up, stabilization, and/or recovery time of a business.

Wallstreet Treadmill: The term used in the industry to describe the strategic inflections in the stock market and/or its effect on real estate values.

Bibliography

The following books have provided much insight and served as a background in the process of writing this book. I have directly quoted from many of them whereas others served as foundational. Unmentioned are many other books, articles, and publications, that served as additional background and research.

Thomas Armstrong; 7 Kinds of Smart, Identifying and Developing Your Many Intelligence's
Penguin Group, New York, NY 1993

This book will transform your thinking about what it means to be smart. It is inspiring, entertaining, and user friendly. This book will help you identify which of the seven intelligence's you are more proficient in and provide you with a checklist of ideas to improve the other intelligence's you have yet to develop. This book has particular value for those that are in pursuit of better understanding themselves and other people. It is equally valuable when you enable the 7 intelligence's to direct your marketing effort. By developing all 7 intelligence's you hit the world's audience intelligently. I highly recommend you consider adding this book to your marketing library.

C. Britt Beemer; Predatory Marketing
William Morrow & Company, New York, NY 1997

Despite its "shocking" marketing cover (a round plate with a furry bunny rabbit on it with a fork on the left of the plate and a knife on the right), I nearly passed this book up. But its predatory title was the hook and its value is the vital research and statistics on buying habits. Its central message is the only way to increase market share is to steal it from the competition and then make them loyal to you. Its value is a subsection called "Fire in the Belly" in Chapter Five (The Vision) and the four characteristics shared by leaders with vision.

Roger Black; Web Sites that Work
Adobe Press 1997

240 full color pages. A real Wow! A compelling experience in the aesthetic delivery of a book. Black, the author, is not just colorful; he and his teams collective works on this project are encouraging for those that desire to design successful web sites that do what you want them to do. Good design means good surfing, exploring, and gathering in a "not insulting of intelligence" way. Cover to cover this book demonstrates how to accomplish this and includes valuable tips such as the "Don't Click Here" strategy.

Jennifer Bothamley; The Dictionary of Theories
Gale Research International LTD. 1993

If you are interested in theories, laws, and principles, you will appreciate this dictionary. The true value of this book is in its indexing, by people and subject. You are sure to find your theory, law or principle without hours and hours of searching. This is the one-stop shop.

W. Steven Brown; 13 Fatal Errors Managers Make and How You Can Avoid Them
Berkley Publishing Group, 1985

Fast and easy reading. The author explains "before we can start managing ourselves we need to stop committing the fatal errors in managing others." Effective and practical in application. A cover to cover value for anyone who manages people.

Steve Bucholz and Thomas Roth; Creating the High Performance Team
John Wiley & Sons, INC. 1987

Filled with case studies, dialogues, and role playing exercises. The team approach must become a management philosophy and apply to the entire work culture. This book demonstrates how to plan and implement the team approach. There is particular value in Chapter Nine (Rapid Response: What opportunities are out there waiting?)

Tom Connellan; Inside the Magic Kingdom, Seven Keys to Disney's Success
Bard Press, Austin Texas, 1996

Fast and easy reading, it is inspirational from cover to cover. It is an inside look at why Disney is such a success. They are the pioneers of staging experiences and the experts at the experience economy. Chapter Six (The Importance of Things Unseen) is of particular value.

Stephen R. Covey; The 7 Habits of Highly Effective People
A Fireside Book Published by Simon & Schuster, 1989

Of the seven principles Habit #4 "Think Win/Win" and Habit #7 "Sharpen the Saw" are of particular interest. Renewal is the principle and the process that empowers toward growth, change and continuous improvement. "Sharpen the Saw" is paramount because it makes all the other habits possible. Everyone should own a copy of this book.

Sam Hill and Glenn Rifkin; Radical Marketing
Harper Collins, New York, NY 1999

Delivers cover to cover radical marketing. It is a must read for those with traditional concepts and those that need affirmation of radicalism to fend off the naysayers. Hill and Rifkin have chosen 10 radical marketers and explain their innovative strategies. The radical history of Harley Davidson, Virgin Airlines, the Grateful Dead, and The Iams Company is interesting and fun.

Eric Hoffer; The True Believer, Thoughts on the Nature of Mass Movements
Harper and Row Publishers, New York, NY 1951

Reveals common peculiarities of mass movements. Religious movements, social revolutions, and nationalist movements are covered in a thought-provoking manner delivering certain essential characteristics in each. It is tough reading but rewarding at its completion. I found the most value in Chapter Fourteen (Unifying Agents) under Persuasion and Coercion.

Edward N. Kelly; Practical Apartment Management Third Edition
Institute of Real Estate Management of the National Association of Realtors First Edition 1976 Third Edition 1990

This book is available through IREM. I received my copy in conjunction with a CPM (Certified Property Manager) course. It is a foundational book for all aspects of apartment management however it is dated from 1990.

Kevin Kelly; New Rules for the New Economy, 10 Radical Strategies for a Connected World
Viking Penguin, 1998

A breakthrough book on the new economy. The 10 rules capture the underlying principles that shape our new economic environment. You understand how networks prosper, how interfaces control attention, and how plentitude drives value. This book is your one-stop shop to the economic future; the author states "the net is our future" and "follow the free."

Jay Conrad Levinson; Guerrilla Marketing, (third edition)
Houghton Mifflin Company 1998

This updated and expanded version identifies the fastest growing markets for the 21st century and how to reach them. Up to date information on the Internet and other technologies is included. Its size is significant and will serve more as a desktop reference to look up strategies rather than cover to cover reading. Particular value is in Chapter 28 (How Guerrilla's use Psychology). You will learn how to access the unconscious mind.

Jay Conrad Levinson; Guerrilla Marketing Attack: New Strategies, Tactics & Weapons For Winning Big Profits From Your Small Business
Houghton Mifflin Company, Boston, MA 1989

If you are a millennium marketer, you should also be a guerrilla. Levinson is brilliant. His books are always packed with ideas and he is attributed to being a "low cost operator." Of all Levinson's books I have enjoyed this one the most. I most valued Chapter Four (From an Art to Science).

Jay Conrad Levinson; Guerrilla Marketing Excellence: The Fifty Golden Rules For Small-Business Success
Houghton Mifflin Company, New York, NY 1993

Although this is a 1993 copyright it is profoundly current. Levinson shares the 50 golden rules with original wit and wisdom. These golden rules will guide your thinking in the process of determining marketing ideas, slogans and campaigns. The most value is in Rule #1 "What the Stonecutter Knows," Rule #3 "What People Really Buy," Rule #33 "Humanity in Marketing," Rule #39 "Achieving Credibility,"and Rule #50 "Eating Life." Even without the other 45 golden rules, this book would be worth reading. Levinson's Epilogue "Breaking the Golden

Rules" is compelling. This is also a must have and will serve as a desktop reference.

Jay Conrad Levinson; Guerrilla Marketing Weapons: 100 Affordable Marketing Methods For Maximizing Profits From Your Small Business
Published by the Penguin Group, 1990

Levinson delivers 100 affordable marketing methods in this book. This arsenal of weapons and firepower is aimed at generating profits. Implement as many as possible, after all, you now have a "Playbook" in which to implement them into.

James L. Lundy; TEAMS "Together Each Achieves More, " How to Develop Peak Performance Teams for World Class Results
Dartnell Corporation, Chicago, IL 1994

Loaded with checklists and outlines for planning, implementing and measuring team effectiveness. This book eloquently defines that there is no "I" in Team. The team concept is foundational and its acknowledgement and practice is paramount.

Edward S. Mckay revised by Arthur M. Rittenberg; The Marketing Mystique
AMACOM, New York, NY 1994

If you are looking for explanations, clarifications, and answers to demystifying the word "Marketing" you will find this book comprehensive and productive. Chapter One of this book (Business: What's It all About)? and Chapter Eight (Marketing Relationships; The Scope of Marketing) are of special interest.

Kathleen McKenna-Harmon & Lawrence C. Harmon; Contemporary Apartment Marketing
Institute of Real Estate Management of the National Association of Realtors 1993

This book is available through IREM. Other than my book this is the only book available on the market that provides an instructional resource for information on real estate "marketing." It is institutional and instructional but does not deliver a "Playbook" and although many of the Chapters are useful, the marketing areas are dated due to a copyright in 1993. McKenna-Harmon and Harmon are leaders. After all they pioneered a book for this industry at a time when it was needed. But the millennium calls for revolutionary changes in marketing.

Regis McKenna; Real Time, Preparing for the Age of the Never Satisfied Customer
Harvard Business School Press—1999

This is the best book on the market to prepare for real time systems and management. It is insightful and provides a practical understanding of how real time plays a key role in customer service. The author delivers the message of real time technology in a compelling and convincing manner; get in real time or get out of business. The real time message summaries at the end of each chapter are of particular value.

David McNally; Even Eagles Need a Push, Learning to Soar in a Changing World
Dell Publishing, a division of Bantam Doubleday, 1990

During turbulent times and weathering many naysayer storms I found solitude in this book. Its value for many will be cover to cover but Chapter Two (The Freedom to Be You) is of particular value. The author explores the choice of career as a vocation. It is in this book that I discovered that marketing is my vocation. In the Latin meaning, the word "vocare" means to call. Marketing is quite possibly a calling for many.

Frederick Newell; The New Rules of Marketing, How to use one-to-one Relationship Marketing to Be the Leader in Your Industry
McGraw-Hill Companies, Inc. 1997

A clear and concise explanation as to why marketing with a database is essential in today's competitive world. It explains how to get started and how to use it. Direct marketing is the underlying premise of this book. If you want a detailed look at direct marketing such as direct mailing as a result of a database targeting strategy, you will find this book useful.

Vance Packard; The Hidden Persuaders
A David McKay Edition Published April 1957

It delivers revealing and often shocking explanations of why we are persuaded to buy and the hidden meanings behind our decisions. It is excellent reading cover to cover but Chapter Seven (Marketing Eight Hidden Needs) is the best reading I have ever come across in only 10 pages. Copywritten in 1957 and now out of print it is still compellingly current in socialistic terms.

William D. Perrault, Jr. and E. Jerome McCarthy; Learning Aid for use with Basic Marketing a Managerial Approach
Richard D. Irwin 1971

Affords complete affirmation that the 4 P's belong to E.J. McCarthy. The real estate industry has borrowed his strategy with great success. This book is the Learning Aid that accompanies the foundational book Basic Marketing. It is a workbook and includes exercises and self-tests. This would be a helpful book for someone who is new to the marketing business.

B. Joseph Pine II and James H. Gilmore; The Experience Economy, Work is Theater and Every Stage is a Business

Harvard Business School Press, Boston MA. 1999

One of the best marketing design covers I have seen yet. The feel and look of the book is an experience in itself. Pine and Gilmore really walk the talk on this one. This is a must read book if you are interested in staging experiences for your customers. For the Leaders, this book is paramount. If you need further exploration of the four stages in the experience economy Chapter Two (Setting the Stage) explains each of them. I highly recommend you consider adding this book to your marketing library.

Paul Postma; The New Marketing Era, Marketing to the Imagination in a Technology-Driven World

McGraw-Hill, New York, NY 1999

A super book for gaining a better understanding of human behavior as the essence of marketing. The introduction is mostly technical, after which the author discusses the relevance in the context of marketing. Chapter Two, the Information Revolution is worth the price of the book alone.

Al Ries and Jack Trout; The 22 Immutable Laws of Marketing

Harper Collins Publishers, INC. 1993

This is a must have book for all marketers. It is a resource that you should not operate without. Law 22, "The Law of Resources" is Ries and Trout's masterpiece and the Warning at the end is of the book is of particular value.

Al Ries and Jack Trout; Positioning, The Battle for your Mind, How to be Seen and Heard in an Overcrowded Marketplace

McGraw-Hill, INC. 1986

"You can position anything" is the central message of this book. Positioning is defined and the authors deliver many positioning strategies used in several industries. The positioning strategies of Xerox, Milk Duds, and the Island of Jamaica, all in Chapters Fourteen, Sixteen, and Seventeen are of particular value. Chapter Two, (The Assault on the Mind) is worth the price of the book alone.

Diane Tracy; The First Book of Common Sense Management
William Morrow & Company, New York, NY 1989

Easy and quick reading. The author asks the question "if good management consists merely of common sense and humanity, why is it so uncommon in the business world today?" The answer is too much fear in the work place. The central message is whether you are a new or experienced manager, you will discover how to show people you care and teach them to do things right the fist time and accomplish this without managing by fear.

Michael Treacy and Fred Wiersema; The Discipline of Market Leaders, Choose Your Customers, Narrow Your Focus, Dominate Your Market
Addison Wesley Publishers Co. 1995

This book is about reinventing the rules of competition to lead the market. The disciplines include the introduction of a risky untested product in lieu of your hottest product, offer a service at a loss to establish loyalty, and link with an adversary to drive costs down. This book explains how to be number one in the market by employing these disciplines. The central message is you can't be all things to all people. Find unique value in your product or offering and deliver it in a chosen market. Chapter Four (The Discipline of Operational Excellence) is the most valuable chapter.

Max Weber; Basic Concepts in Sociology
Carol Publishing Group Edition 1993 original copyright 1962; 1990 by Philosophical Library

Only 123 pages but profound! Weber's central theme is reciprocal social behavior, which becomes a social relation. A social relation is present where individuals base their behavior on the expected behavior of others. Chapter One (On the Concept of Sociology and the "Meaning" of Social Conduct) is of particular interest.

Ron Willingham; The Best Seller! The New Psychology of Selling and Persuading People
Prentice-Hall, INC. Englewood Cliffs, NJ 1984

This book is a road map filled with detailed directions on how to increase your sales. The author delivers a six-step system to persuade customers to listen, trust and then buy from you. Copywritten in 1984, it's dated material; however, there is still much value in the techniques used. This book also delivered another affirmation of the Universal Formula. The books value comes in Chapter Three (How to Find out Where People Hurt so You'll know what Medicine to Prescribe) and in Chapter Ten (How to Get your Customers Saying) "I'm going to buy from you because I like you and trust you."

Zig Zigler; Top Performance, How to Develop Excellence in Yourself and Others
Berkley Publishing Group, New York, NY 1986

Zig Zigler is known as one of the greatest motivational speakers of all time. He is a talented writer and as you read his books you will feel as if he is speaking directly to you. Equal value exists in Chapter Two (Causing Others to Want Your Leadership). There is a simple test to give yourself of significant reasons why others would want to follow you. There is also tremendous value in Chapter One (Choosing to be a Top Performer).

Sergio Zyman; The End of Marketing as We Know It
Harper Collins, New York, NY 1999

Sergio Zyman is a brilliant, passionate, and arrogant marketer. His "in your face" style is challenging, profane, intensely interesting and fun. Zyman defines Marketing as scientific management of experiments and an investment that pays returns. He describes what Marketing is supposed to do and how it can be done. Chapters of particular value are Three (Marketing is Science) Seven (Fish Where the Fish Are) and Ten (I Like Ad Agencies and Some of Them Even Like Me). You will enjoy the cola war stories as well as gain insight on Marketing's single most important function; getting results by selling stuff!

Index

www.ingramcontent.com/pod-product-compliance
Lightning Source LLC
Chambersburg PA
CBHW031050180526
45163CB00002BA/763